AN AFRICA FOR AFRICANS

AN AFRICA FOR AFRICANS

A Plea on behalf of Territorial Segregation Areas and of their Freedom in a South African Colony

BY

ARTHUR S. CRIPPS

WITH A PREFACE
BY
PHILIP KERR, C.H.
Secretary of the Rhodes Trust

WITH MAP

NEGRO UNIVERSITIES PRESS
NEW YORK

Originally published in 1927
by Longmans, Green and Co. Ltd., London

Reprinted 1969 by
Negro Universities Press
A Division of Greenwood Press, Inc.
New York

SBN 8371-2764-5

PRINTED IN UNITED STATES OF AMERICA

To my Friend

JOHN WHITE, W.M.M.S.,

of Mashonaland,

and to that Native Africa of

Wanjanja, Wahera, Waromo and Warozwi,

I have come to know and to love

in these last 26 years—

with Hope

Unconquered and Unconquerable,

rather than with any

confident expectation.

A.S.C.

May, 1927.

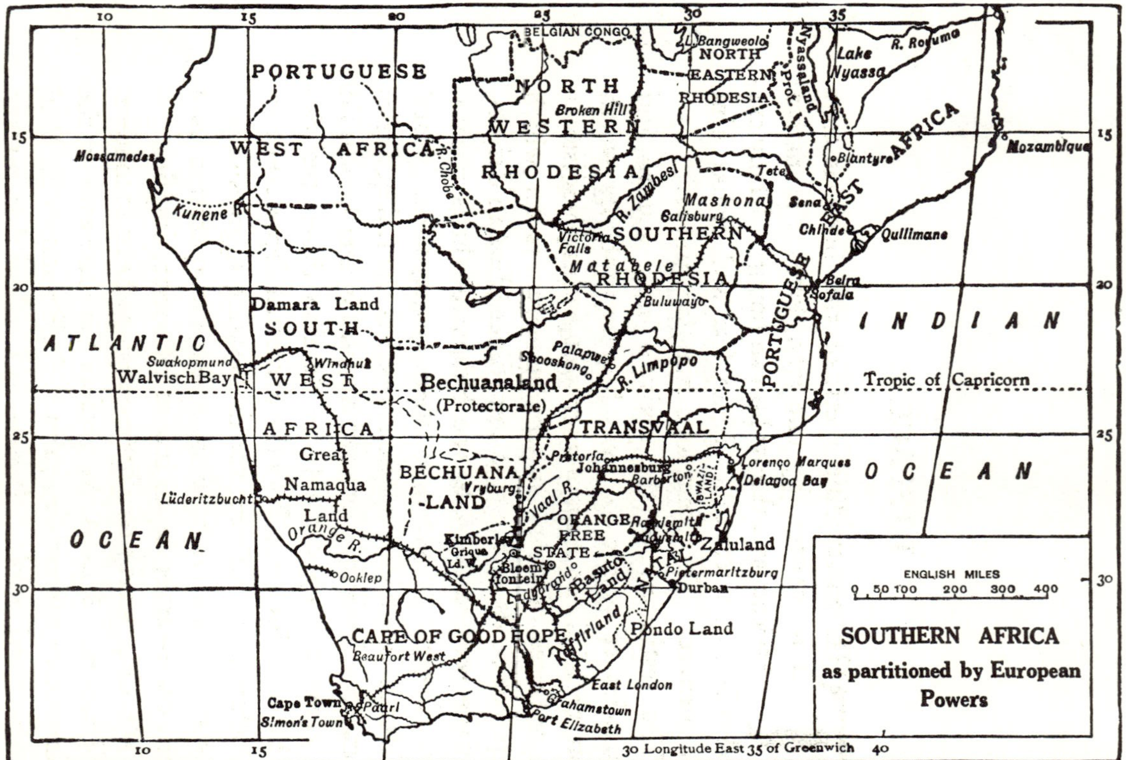

N.B.—The Range, the administrative centre of Charter District, Mashonaland, lies S.W. of Salisbury, about 190 miles from Bulawayo and 90 miles from Salisbury.

PREFACE

THE outstanding merit of this book is that it is written by one who loves the native African as a fellow human being. Many are fond of him as a servant. Many fear and dislike him as a menace. Very few love him for himself.

The testimony to the native's inner nature and capacities of one who loves him is probably worth more than all the measurements of anthropologists or the analyses of those surface appearances on which prejudice feeds : if love is sometimes blind to defects, it alone sees through to the hidden qualities within. Mr. Cripps is satisfied after twenty-three years' residence in Africa that the native has the full qualities of manhood within him, and his plea is that he should be given the opportunity to develop those qualities on his own lines free from the perpetual dependence on the white man and from the dominating aggressiveness of our modern civilization, which incorporation as a mere wage-earner in an industrial society implies.

Mr. Cripps may be a little unsympathetic to modern civilization. I think he prefers the mediæval to the primitive or the modern saint : St. Francis to St. Paul or Abraham Lincoln. Personally I believe that modern democratic civilization, even modern capitalism, has done more to lift the mass of men and women into independence and self-respect and to give them that competence with which they can afford to think of something other than the satisfaction of urgent physical needs than mediæval civilization was able to do. What is needed now is not to destroy it or turn it back but to purify and ennoble it by saving people from making prosperity an end in itself, and by putting back into it that quiet and peace-giving love of spiritual things which is the true end of the civilized life. For all its drab aspects I think that modern Britain can be made into something nobler and better than ever mediæval Britain could have been. The universal simple life on the land, which attracts so many idealists, is only practical where there is more land than people to use it, and a paternal government to protect its inhabitants from invasion, economic as well as political, from without.

I do not share, therefore, Mr. Cripps' half-expressed longing that Africa should be left for Africans alone. White and black have an immense deal to give to one another and, if they can each rise to their opportunities, Africa will contain a better and happier community than if they each struggled along in isolation.

But Mr. Cripps is unquestionably right in his zeal that enough land, good land, should be set aside for native use in those Highlands of Africa which are destined to be colonized by white men, while there is yet time. There is real danger, if this is not done, that the whole native peoples will be depressed by economic forces into a quasi-servile proletariat ministering to a white aristocracy, a result which can only corrupt both black and white, multiply poor whites and poor blacks, and end in revolution and the breaking up of laws. The real protection against this possibility is to give the native ample land on which to develop on lines of his own choosing, to adopt such of the white man's ways as he finds good and to reject the rest, to preserve and develop what is good in his own customs and life instead of having it forcibly crushed out by transplantation, and above all to preserve that peculiar self-respect and freedom which comes from being independent owners of the soil, owning no man as master.

I would go further. There is now a movement everywhere in Africa towards self-government for the white. It seems to me essential that when responsibility is transferred to a local legislature, that legislature should from the start represent all the races settled in the country. In no other way is it possible to avoid the creation of an oligarchy with a vested interest in the maintenance of its own exclusive political power—perhaps the most fruitful cause of injustice to the one race and of degeneration in the other.

Opinions differ as to the way in which Cecil Rhodes' formula "Equal rights for all civilized men" should be applied. Some may cling to the Cape franchise—to the system of high qualifications for the individual voter, but without any differentiation on the score of race or colour. Some may prefer the system of communal representation whereby each community votes for its own representatives. In any case for the present the native in Central African legislatures would have to be represented by white men nominated by the Governor. But what is essential is that from the beginning the political structure of these new and rapidly growing communities should be such as to represent in some way all sections of the community, leaving its development to be moulded later by the light of experience.

PHILIP KERR.

INTRODUCTION

Now, on this Eve of our Precocity,
Ere yet we fumble with an Orb and Crown,
Our Mother England's, feigning they're our own,
Let us not brag what Mighty Men we be,
Nor flaunt Imperial Pomps Imperiously,
Nor, clinking glasses ere the Sun go down,
Swill heady heel-taps of our Sires' Renown!
Homunculi in Lilliput are we.
Nay rather climb this Night some Hill above
Our Breadth of Earth, beneath our Width of sky,
And there (Trade-Patter and Church-Rant put by),
Ask of a Giant Pow'r call'd "God," or "Love,"
That we True Wardens to His Wards may prove
Eight Hundred Thousands of them, You and I!
"Pygmies in Giantdom."

(Lines in Commemoration of the Eve of Responsible Government's Declaration in Mashonaland and Matabeleland on October 1st, 1923.)

IN October, 1923, a British settlers' Responsible Government began its work in Southern Rhodesia. One of the Clauses in its Constitution, the 43rd, enshrined the long-established British principle that a Native may acquire or hold land on the same conditions as a person who is not a Native, that is to say that a Native may buy land anywhere without any legal disqualifications whatsoever. When the conditions of Southern Rhodesia's new Constitution were laid down, the Colonial Secretary for the time being (Mr. Churchill) insisted on Clause 43 being included among them. He, however, expressed himself to this effect :

" In connection with Clause 43, the Rhodesian delegation suggested that specified districts should be set aside by the High Commissioner in which Natives alone might acquire land and within which Europeans should not be allowed to do so. I have informed the delegates that the existing clause enshrines a long accepted principle, and that I should be unwilling to agree to an alteration the corollary of which seems to be the exclusion of Natives from other areas ; but that if full and impartial enquiry should show, after Responsible Government had come into force, that some amendment of the law is necessary, His Majesty's Government would be prepared to consider an amendment."

This expression of opinion has a grave significance, and should help us to realize the importance of Clause 43 as a bulwark of our Southern Rhodesian Commonwealth-in-embryo, and moreover to realize the responsibility that attaches to any movement on our part for its replacement by a Policy intended to secure the Reservation of eligible and adequate Areas in which Natives may find a greater freedom of self-development than they would elsewhere secure.

In January, 1926, a Commission was appointed by His Excellency Sir John Chancellor, Governor of S. Rhodesia, and commissioned to report upon what he had termed " a difficult and delicate operation," this proposed inauguration of an African and European Areas Policy. In the Appendix appended to this book, some attempt to summarize and review the recommendations of this Lands Commission of ours may be found.

Before I make an end here I want to avow my hopefulness as to a Territorial Segregation Policy proving a welcome remedy for our sick sub-continent's racial bitterness, but I am hopeful as to such a Policy, only if it be coupled with a REALLY liberal settlement of our Native Land Question. In a Report to the Government of the South African Union (Blue Book U.G. 41—1918) the late M. Evans, C.M.G., summarized the condition on which a Territorial Separation must depend, if it were to have any real hope of working prosperity. He wrote to this effect :

"The native population is rapidly increasing. By contact and example we are altering their outlook on life. The present generation is not like their fathers, and the next will differ more widely. For a better adjustment in the interests of both races we propose to take away the present right of the native to acquire land where he will, and to strictly limit his opportunities within certain recommended areas. If the scope within such areas is not such as to enable him to reasonably develop with the general progress of the country, then I fear that our attempt will not result in that racial peace and satisfaction which we are attempting to secure."

Granted that saving clause—I avow myself a fervent segregationist at this present critical time in Southern Rhodesia's history. I see the splendid hope of Freedom for the Self-Development of Native Africa, which a Segregation Policy provides at this present juncture when indigenous Native Life is being so hard pressed in our Mixed Areas.

The immediate outlook for our promising Native Races under our present regime of Repressionism for Natives in such Mixed Areas, appears to me to be pathetically squalid and mean. But if Land-Severance and Land-Abundance are to unite, and to form a Dual Alliance for the benefit of our Colony's Natives a real hope of relief may yet be afforded them.

M. Louis Franck has said of Africa : "We want Africa to remain the country we found it, the country which God made, the country of the black peoples, not populated by third-class Europeans, but populated by better Africans."

One who has written on "Race Problems in the New Africa"[1] has told us that to "cover African barbarism with a veneer of European civilization is not a task that is worth any man's while ; but to help Africa to find those elements which she may build up into beautiful manhood and womanhood is a task for which it is worth while to live, or, if necessary, to die."

This book of mine contains many quotations : the writer trusts that any misquotations which may have crept into it may be of minor importance.

A. S. C.

[1] The Rev. W. C. Willoughby, L.M.S.

"And the Lord said, I have surely seen the affliction of my people . . . and have heard their cry . . . for I know their sorrows. . . . And I am come down to deliver them . . . and to bring them up out of that land unto a good land and a large. . . ."

EXODUS iii. 7, 8.

"Come, though the sea be vexed, and breakers
 roar,
Come for the breath of this old world is vile.
Haste we, and toil, and faint not at the oar;
It may be we shall touch the happy isle. . . ."

DE BANVILLE (*Lang's rendering*).

PART I

NOTES ON MIXED AREAS IN SOUTHERN AFRICA AND ON THE MENACE THAT THEY IMPLY TO NATIVE AFRICA'S FREEDOM OF SELF-DEVELOPMENT

INDEX

"If thou seest the oppression of the poor, and violent perverting of judgment and justice in a province, marvel not at the matter: for He that is higher than the highest regardeth; and there be higher than they."—Ecclesiastes v. 8

CHAPTER I

SOUL-ROT IN A SERVILE ATMOSPHERE

CHAPTER I

"As a person in health would not wish to be attended by the sick, nor to have those who live with him to be in a state of sickness, so neither would a person who is free bear to be served by slaves, or to have those who live with him in a state of slavery."
—EPICTETUS.

"NATIVE interests and European interests were irreconcilable. The idea of giving justice to the Natives had never entered the head of white men except a few negrophilists. . . ."

Record of the Speech (commendably protested against at its time of delivery) delivered by a Nationalist Member in the South African Union's Dominion Parliament. *Eastern Province Herald*, 14th July, 1920.

There is a certain far-sighted bequest in the will of Cecil Rhodes which has time and time again fascinated my imagination. I mean his munificent provision for the education of young South African Colonists in the free and idealistic air of Oxford. What is the atmosphere wherein boys of British or Dutch South Africa are normally reared? Opinions are naturally apt to be divergent when such a question comes up for answer. One expert South African authority (an ex-Head Master and a present Coadjutor

Bishop) writes interrogatively as to the South African youths whom he has done so much to educate, and some of whom have played so notable a part in the Great War : " It seems as if there were some capacity for leadership, and if there is, would this be unconnected with the fact that most of these lads had from childhood breathed an atmosphere of command ? " But he admits further on in the essay of his that I have been quoting : " I will not deny that some South Africans are harsh and overbearing, and that a good many are most fierce about race superiority who are least superior."

Another authority, one of perhaps riper experience as to South African race-conflicts, the late Mr. Maurice Evans, C.M.G., has recorded his own view quite candidly : " 'The effect of the possession of power over a people, regarded as inferior, on immature or unbalanced natures may be seen exemplified in the attitude of some white youths towards the natives, whether servants, or dependents, or otherwise.

"There are many exceptions, but too often a domineering and masterful tone is adopted which would be immediately resented by a white man, dependent or not, but which the native puts up with, without outward protest. He is not injured, but the white youth is ; I cannot think that the impunity with which discourteous and inconsiderate acts can be committed is likely to be innocuous[1] to the character in the making of those who follow us."

[1] Cf. Ecclesiastes viii, 9, " . . . there is a time wherein one man ruleth over another to his own hurt."—A.S.C.

I have cited these two authorities with a view to obtaining some sort of an authoritative answer to my question: "What is the atmosphere wherein boys of British or Dutch South Africa are normally reared?" I have, moreover, had opportunities of my own to make certain observations that may help me to an answer. My own conclusion tends to be quite decisive that the prevalent atmosphere of South Africa is neither free nor idealistic, in the senses in which in our English Mother Country we have been taught to understand those words. And, in the nature of things, what else can we expect, the South African Dominion's failure to prove herself a commonwealth[1] to all the races that inhabit her, having been in these last years so obvious? An inveterate habit of refusing to face facts has obsessed South Africa in these last significant years.

Church and State for the most part seem to agree in ignoring the inconsistencies of a peace that is no peace in their overlapping provinces. "The thing that hath been it is that which shall be."[2]

The vested interests of both Church and State, here shallowly conceived and short-sightedly estimated, seem to be identified with the cheerless fatalism

[1] "... I can perceive nothing but a certain conspiracy of rich men procuring their own commodities under the name and title of the commonwealth."—Sir Thomas More, "The Second Book of Utopia."

"The white man ... is determined to do all he can to remain and, what is more, to rule. ... This matter is to us in South Africa such a vital and fundamental matter that no ethical considerations, such as the rights of man ... will be allowed to stand in the way. ..." Sir Thomas Watt in *The Times*, March 30th, 1926.

[2] Ecclesiastes i, 9.

expressed in that text which I have just quoted from Ecclesiastes. The demand for toleration, or even approval, of unjust traditions being so powerfully voiced as it is by those in power here, is it not likely that a supply will meet such a demand, human nature being what we know it to be ?

It is well then surely that from such a highly artificialized conservatory as our South African sub-continent, a certain number of aspirants, young, and presumably still impressionable, should be helped to escape into the open air of research and enquiry, which Oxford may be relied upon to afford them. Let us welcome Rhodesia's Founder's bequest for linking up South Africa with his own University as a bequest supplementing his plain pronouncement with regard to equal rights for every civilized man south of the Zambesi ! The bequest and the pronouncement taken together constitute assuredly their begetter's finest claim to the lasting respect of true Imperialists. Imagine a young Anglo-African deeply versed in the restricted views of his own near relations, or locally venerated pastors and teachers, let loose on Burke and Shelley and Mill, not to name any more modern upholders of the same British tradition that these classic names represent !

Will those of the generations following our own observe some belated yet fruitful working of Oxford leaven in the Africander lump ? I, for one, am hopeful that they may. Meanwhile the present outlook with regard to civic felicity in South Africa (albeit most certainly relieved by such glimmering[1] of vistas as the Native Affairs Bill of 1920 has opened out before the Union's Natives) is dark indeed. What do I mean by civic felicity? I am writing with two lines of our English Spenser ringing in my memory:

> "What more felicity can fall to creature
> Than to enjoy delight with liberty?"

There is certainly to be found in the ruling races of present-day South Africa a passionate resentment against interference with their own liberties. But it is too often exemplified in defence of their capricious claim to circumscribe the delights of liberty for their subject races.[2] The delight in liberty, not claimed for a caste of one's own exclusively, but inclusively for a commonwealth whereto one and all belong, where is that to be found as a civic possession in South Africa? Possibly within the Crown Protectorates, Basutoland and her sisters, in a modified sense. Certainly nowhere else so far as I know.

Some Christian mediævalists, I suppose, may be found to rejoice over the state of the body politic in modern South Africa. Demonstrably there is to be

[1] A glimmering between the blacknesses of years 1913 and 1926, when the Native Land Bill and the Colour Bar Bill achieved, each in its turn, the Union Parliament's sanction.

[2] Southern Rhodesian attempts to refuse a Native's application for a brick-maker's plot, and to refuse a Native motor driver's licence may be noted.

The Preface of W. C. Scully's "Daniel Varenna" (dated 1922) gives a quaint story of Durban's division of labour and the rewards of labour. Europeans were employed at 10s. a day to paint the lower sections of standards carrying electric wires, a simple task and not dangerous. Natives were employed for the painting of the upper sections, for which work a certain amount of skill was wanted, and in which work there was danger of death from contact with live wire, their rate of pay being 1s. 6d. per day.

found scope therein for the anachronistic exercise of benevolent exploitation[1] and repression by an unquestioned soi-disant Christian autocracy. In its privileged annexation of land and land's prerogatives, a proletariat, still to a vast extent illiterate and pagan, acquiesces as a mere matter of course. Moreover, in up-to-date Africa, there is to be found a congenial sphere for the exercise of stringent as well as sympathetic authority by those classes of Christian ministers and religious corporations whose interferences and encroachments have been so liable to be swept aside elsewhere. In States that have moved with the times further than South Africa has done, the streams of modern thought have long had torrential force, for good as well as for evil—a force that South Africa has not yet had to reckon with. Not for a long time now has the supply of cheap exploitable labour maintained its old standards of docility and tractability in Europe.

What wonder then if Africa offers unique attractions nowadays to European reactionaries alike for their immigration and for their investments? The entrenched system of old Europe need not now fear in the vast acreages of South and East Africa any speedy dislodgment, having once dug itself so securely in, as it has already succeeded in doing. The normal rate of progress in South-East Africa (that pace-of-the-ox region) gives full assurance that Europe's vested

[1] I have seen a *compulsory* assessment card issued under the auspices of a certain Mission (Males 4s. od., Females 2s. od.) inscribed with words in a Native language which signified, "Ye have been given much: give much!" Surely a not very scholarly or exact rendering of Our Lord's appeal for *free* gifts—"Freely ye have received: freely give!" Or "Gratis ye have received: gratis give!"—A.S.C.

interests need fear no lack of interested admirers, *laudatores temporis acti*, for many a long year yet. In Africa, Reaction has indeed found harbourage from post-War storms—a haven where it would be.

Nevertheless, whatsoever defence might be reasonably urged long ago for such a system as still obtains there, the system from the point of view of civic felicity has been long indefensible. Indefensible or not, it survives with fine promise of longevity into our own time, to the detriment of our commonwealth. Be it remembered that we are nearly two thousand years on in the Christian era, and that the French Revolution (with its sequel of emancipation from slavery) is long gone by. Yet here and nowadays in this South Africa of ours, languor broods as it did aforetime, languor by no means incompatible with a ghoulish vigour of self-interest.[1] "They should tell him," said a Member of South Africa's Dominion Parliament, speaking of the Native-born in South Africa (no longer ago than 1913, when the South African Native Land Act was under discussion), "as the Free State told him, that it was a white man's country, that he was not going to be allowed to buy land there or hire land there, and that if he wanted to be there he must be in service."[2] If the aforesaid Measure, passed in the form

[1] In "South Africa" for March 19th, 1926, it is written: "The Natives of the Union are protesting against the new taxes they are called on to pay. A Native minding sheep and receiving only 5s. per month has to hand to the Tax Collector £1 10s., equivalent to an income tax of 50 per cent."

[2] By passing the Bill, the Government conceded all the extravagant demands of the "Free" Staters; yet, a year later they took up arms against the Government. ("Native Life in South Africa," by Solomon Plaatje.)

in which it was, has not entirely satisfied the root-and-branch convictions of such an out-spoken repressionist, it has most assuredly gone far to satisfy them. As a Southern Rhodesian, who dreads instinctively the threatened commitment of nine hundred thousand South Rhodesian Natives to the tender mercies of the Union that passed such an Act, I would recall certain words that an English journal printed some years ago. Its correspondent wrote[1]: "But here in South Africa on the day the 'Act' came into law . . . thousands of the natives found themselves ruined and homeless. From tenants they became serfs." He went on to contend that "British justice" and "Russian tyranny" might be regarded as synonymous terms amongst the intelligent and thoughtful of our subject races.

So much for the ghoulish vigour of self-interest; let us return to the languor! Anglo-Africa is surely singularly listless and irresponsive to culture in the broader sense, to Art, to Letters, to Christian Ethics, if not to Christian formularies. May not certain reasons for her listlessness be quite plausibly assumed? From the point of view of the religion of Jesus, she lives a lie. From the point of view of Britain's traditional passion against all repression, and of Britain's inherited zeal for liberty in self-development, she is a traitress glorying in the shame of her own treason. As to her professed passion for democracy, have we not been enlightened recently as to the real definition

[1] Mr. Advocate F. A. Silva, writing in an English newspaper, *The Daily News*.

of so-called democracy in South Africa? Is it not "the rule of a small minority over a vast majority, the rulers naturally (things being what they are) looking after their own interests first?"[1]

As one who has for long periods breathed the air of South Africa, tainted as it is with colour prejudice, fouled with the reek of illogical privilege, and unwarranted prerogative, I plead, in all solemnity, for any real opening-up of any fair way of extrication yet available. That a generous scheme of Segregation,[2] generous in reality not pretence, as to the apportionment of the whole land south of the Zambesi between its inhabitants, European, Eurafrican, African or Asiatic—such a scheme as was worked out in the book I have already quoted, Evans' "Black and White in South-East Africa"—may provide such a way of extrication, I verily believe.

> "There's a divinity that shapes our ends,
> Rough hew them how we will."

The rough surgery of such an honest attempt as I have indicated may at least be well worth trial with a view to earning the Divine blessing of a moral

[1] "The Socialist—the Labour man—is in a curious position in South Africa. If he styles himself a Socialist, he must qualify his attitude to the extent of excluding from his humanity those millions who most desperately need it. If he styles himself a Labour man, he must specifically act against the interests of the very people, who . . . are the real workers in the land."—Mrs. S. G. Millin—"The South Africans."

[2] Dr. S. M. Molema (in "The Bantu—Past and Present") is candid as to segregation. He says: "But first and foremost, THE SEPARATION MUST BE EQUITABLE. Such a just, fair, and equitable separation can alone provide the privileges of self-government, and free constitutional life to black and white."

Surely he espies a hope in such segregation, if only a very frail hope, for all South Africa.

recovery for the nation that attempts it. What did Evans himself have to say in recommendation of his own scheme? Amongst his arguments we may find this notable one: "For the white man it will mean much to his inner life."

Any such expedient surely is well worth the trying if thereby we be delivered from the body of our present civic death—our present evangelistic atrophy. Sins of omission and commission against ruled and subject peoples are grave enough matters in this epoch of racial self-consciousness—an epoch of such resonant protestations as were made within the limits of our recent wartime—a time when it suited even rulers and exploiters to make them.

But what of the tragedy of the present generation of Anglo-Africans living, so to speak, a life of mortal sin against the Commonwealth, and jealously demanding their own innocent children's right to live it after them? "And if one look unto the land . . . the light is darkened in the heavens thereof." "A wonderful and horrible thing is committed in the land; the prophets[1] prophesy falsely, and the priests bear rule

[1] Many things that have long wanted saying about the unsatisfactoriness of Christian witness up-to-date, as well in South Africa as East Africa, are said concisely and clearly by Dr. Norman Leys in his Preface to the 3rd Edition of "Kenya." One or two extracts must suffice here: "In the text of this book the opinion is expressed that Protestant foreign missions are at the parting of the ways. There are increasing signs that the whole movement is, like so many similar movements in the past, taking the wrong road and departing with increasing certainty from the plans and ideals of the founder of the Christian religion. . . . There is the very greatest need for every supporter of missions to realize that the same fate that overwhelmed the Franciscans and all those others of our precursors who in spite of lying priests and false prophets have kept the spark in Christianity alive, also threatens this movement of our time, so that what once was the creative inspirer of a new order of society is being turned into a mere prop of

by their means, and my people love to have it so : and what will ye do in the end thereof ? "

It is well assuredly if men in this lovely South Africa of ours find enlightenment, even if they should have to go far on pilgrimage, even as far as Oxford,[2] to seek it. Enlightenment as to the existence of wrongs in their own midst (for the continuance of which they themselves can be held largely responsible and called to a stern account, if not now then at some future date), may prove to be a precious boon, well worth a pilgrimage, to South Africa's present-day pilgrims.

It is ill assuredly if enlightenment as to such injuries should breed in our South African stay-at-homes a sort of blind resentment against the injured. Has not one of our modern novelists[3] defined " the hatred of the injurer for the injured " as " one of the few things in the world that are pure black, and have no ray or reflection of any good, however inverted or distorted, in them " ?

the existing order." Nevertheless the old Philo-African tradition of the Christian Church has been gloriously maintained by certain individuals and groups of devoted twentieth-century missionaries (e.g., Frank Weston of the Universities Mission to Central Africa, John White of the Wesleyan Methodist Mission in Mashonaland, and those alliances of South African clergymen which have ruffled the judicial calm of the South African Union's Minister of Justice quite recently).

[2] Cf. "The Autobiography of Kingsley Fairbridge" [Oxford Univ. Press.]

[3] E. F. Benson.

CHAPTER II

POSTULATES IMPERILLED

CHAPTER II

"In those days which men reck not of now, man, when he hungered, fed on the flesh of his fellow man and found it sweet. Yet even in those days it came to pass that there was one whose head was higher than her fellows and her thought keener, and as she picked the flesh from a human skull, she pondered."
—OLIVE SCHREINER.

A POSTULATE is at the back of much of the trouble in South Africa. This Postulate takes for granted that there is something defective about the African Native as a man, and that, in consequence, his rights as a man are open to dispute.

Much might be written on the uses, not to say the abuses of the Postulates' long-lived line. "The King can do no wrong!" "My country—right or wrong!" "Discipline must be maintained!"—these may serve as examples of the Postulate—that formidable and prolific breed. Have not these and such-like assumptions furnished forth in our midst a sort of standing Reserve Force—standing to arms promptly when questions are to be begged, or argument is to be precluded? Has not that Force taken its mobilization orders from Vested Interests not infrequently? Have not those Interests owed life and length of days to its creed of No Surrender?

It may be that the old-fashioned Postulate's prestige is not quite what it used to be in the Old Country. Decay of its reputation there, at the heart of things, in an age of interrogations, need cause us little astonishment. Many a scarecrow, that in its fluttering prime saves a bird-scarer's wages, may become, ere its day of supersession overtakes it, a byword for futility.

Father Time, in his recurrent lapses, is apt to beget Sophistication, that born foe and relentless interrogator of elderly Postulates.

In Anglo-Africa, where one has lived so long, such Postulates have been called up, to one's own knowledge, for many spells of Active Service, and have enjoyed no transient vogue and no fleeting reputation. South Africa's comparative isolation has tended to prolong the reigns of South Africa's old-fashioned Postulates. Nevertheless in our obscure part of the world Time has lapsed, as elsewhere, and Sophistication has been begotten within the confines, and amongst the conservatories, of South Africa. Strange to relate, even in this Southern Rhodesia of ours, where certain hoary and cherished Postulates have not only found sanctuary, but have dominated and dictated, with comparatively little opposition, ever since Eighteen-Ninety's Occupation days, a sophisticated Inquisitor has at last appeared. In his book, "The Black Man's Place in South Africa," published in 1923,[1] a Rhodesian writer has subjected

[1] "The Black Man's Place in South Africa," published by Messrs. Juta & Co., of Cape Town.

certain Postulates (full of years, and of honour, be it said) to the abashless Inquisition of modern research.

Mr. Peter Nielsen, now a Native Commissioner in Mashonaland, can produce fine credentials for this self-appointed task of his as Grand Inquisitor. He has been doing magisterial work in an asbestos-mining district, he has acted as interpreter of the Court in Bulawayo, he claims in his Preface to know the Natives' language as well as they do themselves. He brings to his work not only the qualifications of a book-student, but also of one who has amassed by dint of experience much relevant information.

He applies himself first and foremost to the finding of an answer for one particular question, which he states as follows : " Is the African Native equal to the European in mental and moral capacity, or is he not ? "

He says : " We must have an answer to this question, for we cannot assign to the Native his proper place in the general scheme of our civilization till we know exactly what manner of man he is.

" We of to-day are rightly proud of our freedom from the sour superstitions and religious animosities of the past, but these hindrances to progress and general happiness were only dispelled by the light of scientific thought and clear reasoning. Let us then bring to bear that same blessed light upon our present enquiry into reasons, real or fancied, for those prejudices of race and colour which we still retain, for it is only by removing the misconceptions and false notions that obscure our view that we can come to a clear understanding of the many complex issues that make up the great Native problems of South Africa."

Under the heading of "Bodily Differences," Mr. Nielsen's battue of our South Africa Postulates begins in earnest. As to the "belief, at one time commonly held, that in morphological development and physical appearance the Bantu stands nearer in the scale of evolution to our common ape-like ancestors than do the white people," Mr. Nielsen enlightens us to the following effect—"Careful investigation by trained observers all over the world have shown that the various simian features discernible in the anatomy of modern man are found fairly evenly distributed amongst advanced and backward races." "Extreme hairiness of body . . . is seldom met with in the Bantu, but is equally common among Europeans and Australian aboriginals. . . ." "The texture also of the African's hair is less like that of the hair of the man-like apes than is the hair of the European. The proportions of the limbs of the Europeans seem, on the average, to be nearer to the supposed prototype of man than those of the Bantu."

Another Postulate, that had become quite popular amongst us, is discredited by Mr. Nielsen—"If there is a thing which the white man of South Africa is sure about it is the comparative thickness of the 'nigger skull', but this notion also would appear to be one of the many which have no foundation in fact." The opinion of medical men, based upon actual observation and measurement, is to the effect that there is no evidence to support the contention that the Native skull is thicker than that of the European. Mr. Nielsen points out that the thickness and texture of the Native's hair " may account for his supposed comparative invulnerability to head injuries. . . ." He reminds us that the layman observer " is more often given to vehement assertion than to careful enquiry."

He goes on to grapple with another hardy Postulate which concerns the supposed " arrest of the brain of the Bantu at the age of puberty owing to the closing of the sutures of the skull at an earlier age than happens to Europeans. . . ." He tells us that the opinion of modern authorities on this popular notion " is that those who say that the closure of the sutures of the skull determines brain growth would or should also say that the cart pulls the horse, for, if the sutures of the Native skull close at a somewhat earlier date in the average Native than in the average European, then it simply means that the Native reaches maturity slightly earlier than the average white man." He argues, moreover, that " the loss of mental alertness, said by some to be peculiar to the Natives at the time of puberty, is very often met with in the European youth and girl at the same time of life." " Competent observers," he tells us, " have of late come to the conclusion that this supposed falling-off in intelligence, in so far as it may differ in degree from what has so often been noticed in European boys and girls at that point of development, is due to psychological and not to physiological causes." He explains that what is meant is that the tendency to mind-power's deterioration in the young European is checked by force of example and other factors, "all of which factors are as yet seldom present in the surroundings of the average Bantu boy or girl." His conclusion is that—"The outward ethnic differentiæ of the Bantu are admittedly palpable and patent to everyone, but in the opinion of competent observers there is nothing in the anatomy of the black man to make him a lower beast than the man with the white skin."

Considerations of space forbid one to follow out closely here Mr. Nielsen's further contentions as to "The mind of the Native," and as to his lack of opportunity (through stress of isolation) having militated against the Native's achievement in former generations. Nor has the time come yet to quote in full his impassioned and well-justified plea for the provision of ample Native Areas, wherein the Bantu, *apart from the European's undue interference*, may be able to develop on his own lines that which Providence has implanted in him. "With freedom of movement and action under a minimum of European supervision and control the Natives will, in their own areas, have full opportunity and scope for the development of a home-civilization of their own along lines similar to, if not identical with, those by which the Europeans follow their separate ways."

In the later pages of his treatise, Mr. Nielsen allows little quarter to certain dogmas much-beloved of white Africa,[1] that concern Africa's black inhabitants.

[1] "'Treat an African decently and as a human being, and in ninety-nine cases out of a hundred he will behave like one.' In this matter Major Lloyd-Jones criticizes very strongly a large part of the British settlers in Kenya Colony. Not only, he says, do they regard the native

(Need I specify the sort of dogmas I have in mind?) He tells us how he has himself endeavoured to show that there is good reason for believing the Bantu to be no less capable of adopting and adapting Western civilization than other races which in the past have risen from rude barbarism to high culture, but here, says he, "I admit that the full proof of my belief must be given by the Natives themselves." Dark though the racial outlook in Southern and Eastern Africa may be as yet, Mr. Nielsen's face at least has the light on it, for it is turned eastwards towards the dawn of realization "that we cannot set artificial barriers in the way of the civilized Native if he proves that he has the capacity for going higher and the will to try." He is a devotee of the New Learning: he is out to teach his fellow European to treat his African contemporary "not as a slave nor as a child, nor yet as a brother in the house, but as a man. The Native can in fairness demand no more, the whites can in fairness yield no less." Was not the late Theodore Roosevelt right in naming "aggressive fighting for the right" as the noblest sport the world afforded? Have not those well-preserved big-game of South Africa, her racial Postulates, yielded Mr. Nielsen some noble sport already? Then in the name of our common Humanism or Christianity, let us wish him "Good Hunting!" Moreover, let us hear Mr. Nielsen further as to his main contention:

contemptuously as a 'nigger,' but they believe him to be merely a beast of burden, and are much surprised that they have little success with the Masai, a fighting race. . . ." Review in *Times' Lit. Supplement*, 6th January, 1927.

" I am no encomiast of the Natives, for I know them to be no better than other people, but search as I may, I cannot find that Native character which is alleged to be inherently different from the white man's character, is so. Did not Mark Twain find, as the most conspicuous result of his travels, that ' there is a good deal of human nature everywhere,' and is it not true that human nature is everywhere the same ? "

Once upon a time a prophetess, who was named Olive Schreiner, wrote about Mashonaland wherein the present writer has made his home. She wrote in a very dark time nearly a generation ago. Into the mouth of her Christ in Mashonaland she put this parable of dawn's inevitability : " To-morrow's sun shall rise . . . and it shall flood these dark kopjes with light, and the rocks shall glint in it. Not more certain is that rising than the coming of that day. And I say unto you that even here in the land where now we stand . . . where an acre of gold is worth a thousand souls, and a reef of shining dirt is worth half a people, even here that day shall come."[1]

Now that this book, " The Black Man's Place in South Africa " has been published, I hail the promise of our Territory's daybreak. The night of that Territory may be still too dark for clear sight, but the grim black of some of her Postulates has become grey, and lets the light through already, so to speak. One is tempted to regret that the book I have just quoted

[1] Compare that proclamation of a Divine challenge to the Ancient World's Imperialism : " I will make a man more precious than fine gold ; even a man than the golden wedge of Ophir."—Isaiah xiii, 12.

was not published only two or three years earlier in time for our prophetess to have hailed it with a "NUNC DIMITTIS, DOMINE," or ever she was laid to rest in that Anglo-Dutch Africa of ours to which she preached the love of the brethren—the love whose adoption means nothing less than the passing from death unto life.

CHAPTER III

THE LURE OF DISPOSSESSION

CHAPTER III

> "If 'twere a cabin in the green sad Isle,
> Or crofter's cottage on red heather ground,
> Would you not sigh? But being what it is,—
> A Kaffir's hut the granite hills hedge round
> With bins and byre for corn and cattle his,
> Why need you sigh if it be giv'n away
> Over his heathen head, and he must pay,
> Or leave his home? Should you not rather smile
> With yonder Christians out to make their pile?"
>
> "A Million Acres."

> "There were two men in one city; the one rich, and the other poor."—2 Samuel xii, 1.

I REMEMBER once in Mashonaland being confronted with an alluring announcement of South African farming prospects. The announcement was to this effect: "Some so-called South African farms are really delightful estates. . . . No career is more absorbing than planning and evolving, as through the centuries so many in Britain have done, a landed estate for one's family; it gives one a definite objective in life, something tangible in these days of uncertainty and difficulty. Hence the growing land-hunger." After a significant reminder, "Capital is necessary," the reader was referred for fuller information to a publicity agent at the London Office of the High Commissioner for the Union of South Africa.

An opinion of the late Maurice Evans recorded in

his " Black and White in South East Africa " flashes into one's mind as relevant to such alluring inducements. In his sketch of a proposed reformation of land facilities, so far as those facilities might be made available in a practicable scheme for the Union of South Africa's Native inhabitants, he makes this pathetic admission : " It is quite possible that, when investigation has been made and everything done to provide land sufficient for the home-life of the native people, a surplus number may remain for whom no provision is possible. In any case, for the many thousands who reside on occupied farms in Natal and the Transvaal, it will be impossible to find land in native areas for years to come."[1] We may then conclude, from a consultation of these two authorities cited by me, that, in one of our self-governing British Dominions, to wit the Union of South Africa, there is land and to spare for the building-up of immigrant capitalists'[2] big estates, while, on the other hand, the provision of suitable land for the peasant culture of aboriginal Africans presents an ominous difficulty. One is reminded of a maxim of Burke's in his reflections on the French Revolution :

" The body of the people must respect the property of which they cannot partake. They must labour

[1] Since this South African publicist wrote, much has happened in South Africa. At the International Africa Conference held in Belgium (September, 1926) Professor Macmillan said : " Whites in South Africa tend to forget, or do not know that even now hardly half the Native population have any roots in the land. . . ."

[2] " Empire Settlement " issued by the Church of England Council of Empire Settlement informs me with regard to South Africa, that the " 1820 Memorial Settlers' Association offers a free course of training to intending settlers with some capital."—A.S.C.

to obtain what by labour can be obtained ; and when they find, as they commonly do, the success disproportioned to the endeavour, they must be taught their consolation in the final proportions of eternal justice."

It was only little by little, and dimly as well as slowly, that I learned particulars of the divorce between labourers and land brought about in pre-Reform Bill England. Then at last in the Hammonds' comprehensive treatise on "The Village Labourer," I came upon an abundance of particulars sifted and set in order—tragic order moving to its due conclusions, alike of pity and of scorn.

In the Southern and Eastern Africa of my own day I have seen history repeating itself on the deplorable lines of that now long accomplished divorce in old England. As we puzzle over our problems about land and labourers in Britain overseas, it would be well if we attended to the warnings which that ancient transaction, recorded in our Mother Country's domestic history, has bequeathed to us. I for one am glad to have had certain lessons in old English rural history afforded to me by my own experiences, as well as by books. Such lessons have, I hope, helped to intensify my protest against the thing that hath been in old Britain repeating itself, and reproducing itself, before my very eyes in this new Britain of my adoption.

I was born and brought up in a Kentish town, but went to work amongst East Sussex labourers early in the 'nineties. As I look back upon information gathered, from one and another, in my sphere of work, I see that I was helped to realize what a distressful drama had been staged in its local history somewhere about the year 1830, when smuggling and sheep-stealing were apparently rampant. In the inn, where I once lodged, with a window of mine looking out on Dungeness Point, a man deeply involved in the latter business was said to have lived. I remember, too, how an old lodger in our parish told me of his own experience as a smuggler ; his brother had been shot, and was buried in our village churchyard. The vicarage, moreover, had its own tradition of a shot through the window in the old troublous times, when the vicar, who had opposed smuggling, providentially escaped. The grouping of alleged cause and alleged effect in an era of rural violence[1] was hidden from my eyes in my curate days. But I do not doubt that my fire of sympathy for a country labouring population found plenty of fuel in Sussex. I seem to remember a very old woman (a labourer's wife) who lived, when I knew her, not far from Icklesham village, telling me how she had had but eightpence a week in wages after providing for her household's allowance of flour. I suppose that the date of her stern struggle may have been in " the hungry 'forties " or thereabouts. I remember that I agreed to sign a memorial from certain clergy (an Archbishop commented on the junior status of many of its signatories) deploring the apparent want of

[1] It is no wonder that in the early nineteenth century there was an outbreak of crime in the English country. Gangs of thieves, made up of labourers, some artisans, and even a few small farmers broke into corn-lofts and barns and were able to sell their booty."—" The Making of Rural Europe," by H. Irvine.

enthusiasm shown on our Bishops' Bench for that charter of the villages—the Parish Councils' Bill. Not long afterwards I was put in charge of a small rural parish in Essex—a parish the church and vicarage of which, built in or about the early 'seventies, had already cracked uneasily. Rumour spoke of a curse lowering over that church's site. I am inclined to admit that this area quite probably formed part of a comparatively recent enclosure which had annexed village common-land. Its troubles, caused by stiff clay's contractions in dry seasons may, or may not, have been reinforced by the bias of an ill-gotten origin. In any case the problem of its stability remained acute for many years. Whilst I was in Essex a Red Van visited one of the Greens in the neighbouring parish of Felstead, and I gave myself as a recruit to its mothering body, the Land Restoration League. Now the Land Restoration League, as I understand its main drift, stood for the principle, or pious aspiration, that the land of England should belong, or should be restored, to the Commonweal of England. How much more truly, at no very distant date before the French-War-period enclosures took place, the land had belonged to the Commonweal of England than it did at the close of the nineteenth century, I was to learn later on. Before, however, this occurred, I was to make my own home for years on an African Native Reserve, or in its neighbourhood, and to see for myself the communal tribal life of African agriculturists and stock-owners, a life lived in close dependence upon their mother soil. Moreover, I was to see that life of theirs threatened with encroachments, if not with supersession, as the advancing tide of colonists' land-settlement made its way into the part of Africa where I lived, and the consequent expropriation of Africans' mother soil proceeded. What that expropriation may mean, one[1] who used to be a Northern Rhodesian Missionary, has explained in words of memorable pathos : " A new site can never be the same to the people, for African religion is rooted in the soil, and bound to the parcel of ground hallowed by the presence of the dead. One needs to hear the pagan African's lament as to the piteous condition of their deceased parents and chiefs reduced to misery by the enforced migration of their subjects and children, in order to understand the firm attachment of the people to their land. Separation from their land means a severance between the 'dead' and the 'living' members of the community, with an inevitable slackening of the moral obligations which that communion entailed."

Intuitively and instinctively I am inclined to champion the old order of things in Africa against the tendencies of new conditions to menace it unfairly. But it seems to me that I have found what appear to be valid arguments in support of my intuitions and instincts, arguments drawn from a not very remote period of Great Britain's history.

I cannot give a better idea of how the divorce between English land and English labour was brought

[1] The Revd. Edwin W. Smith (the quotation is from an article in " The East and the West." The passage reappears slightly changed in " The Golden Stool.")

about than by transcribing three or four passages from J. L. and Barbara Hammond's "The Village Labourer."

I take, first, a passage that indicates the vast difference that the change made:

"At the time of the great Whig revolution, England was in the main a country of commons and of common fields; at the time of the Reform Bill England was in the main a country of individualist agriculture and of large enclosed farms."

Secondly, I want to find a passage that gives some sane rationale of those motives, fair and not so fair, that swayed and bent men's minds to engineer and accept such a momentous change. The following statement seems to embody something of the kind that I want:

"The agricultural community which was taken to pieces in the eighteenth century and reconstructed in the manner in which a dictator reconstructs a free government, was threatened from many points. It was not killed by avarice alone. . . . A dictatorship lends itself more readily than any other form of government to the quick introduction of revolutionary ideas, and new ideas were in the air. . . . Many an enclosing landlord thought only of the satisfaction of doubling or trebling his rent: that is unquestionable. If we are to trust so warm a champion of enclosure as Sir William Marshall, this was the state of mind of the great majority. But there were many whose eyes glistened as they thought of the prosperity they were to bring English agriculture, applying to a wider and wider domain the lessons that were to be learnt from the processes of scientific farming. . . ." The spirit in which the Board of Agriculture approached the subject found appropriate expression in Sir John Sinclair's high-sounding language : " The idea of having lands in common, it has been justly remarked, is to be derived from that barbarous state of society, when men were strangers to any higher occupation than those of hunters or shepherds, or had only just tasted the advantages to be reaped from the cultivation of the earth."

With that passage should be read this very significant one, embodying the grudge that the few seem to have felt against the way in which the old rural system had defied and defeated their will-to-power in rural parishes—Mr. Bishton, who wrote the " Report on Shropshire," in 1794, gives a still more interesting glimpse into the mind of the enclosing class : " The use of common land by labourers operates upon the mind as a sort of independence." When the commons are enclosed[1] " the labourers will work every day in the year, their children will be put to labour early, and that subordination of the lower ranks of society which in the present times is so much wanted would be thereby considerably secured."

[1] Cf. Lord Olivier's words in his " Master and Man in the Tropics " essay. " Moreover, every native in the established social system of Africa, and every West Indian cultivator who, or whose family, owns or occupies land, has a great many other things to do and to think of than the earning of a day's wage by means of regular work. He sees no merit in this, when the demands outrun his own convenience ; and as a matter of fact any such habit would interfere with and destroy his own mode of life. It is only suitable to a landless proletariat divorced from the instruments of industry, and which, after earning its living wage, has nothing else to do than to buy things with it in shops to keep the family going till next pay day."

Lastly I would quote a passage that makes clear how pitiful the results of such sweeping changes were apt to be, and how unfavourably on the whole the trend of rural affairs in old England compared with that in old France, strange news as that may sound to many of us.

"The petitions that are buried with their brief and unavailing pathos in the 'Journals' of the House of Commons are the last voice of village independence, and the unnamed commoners who braved the dangers of resistance to send their doomed protests to the House of Commons that obeyed their lords were the last of the English peasants. These were the men, it is not unreasonable to believe, whom Gray had in mind when he wrote :

> 'Some village Hampden that with dauntless breast
> The little tyrant of his fields withstood.'

"As we read the descriptions of the state of France before the Revolution, there is one fact that comforts the imagination and braces the heart. We read of the intolerable services of the peasant, of his forced labour, his confiscated harvests, his crushing burdens, his painful and humiliating tasks. . . . The peasant may be overwhelmed by the dime, the taille, the corvée, the hundred and one services that knit his tenure to the caprice of a lord : he may be wretched, brutal, ignorant, ill-clothed, ill-fed, and ill-housed : but he has not lost his status : he is not a casual figure in a drifting proletariat: he belongs to a community that can withstand the seigneur, dispute his claims at law, resume its rights, recover its possessions, and establish, one day, its independence.

"In England the aristocracy destroyed the promise of such development when it broke the back of the peasant community. The enclosures created a new organization of classes. The peasant with rights and a status, with a share in the fortunes and government of his village, standing in rags, but standing on his feet, makes way for the labourer with no corporate rights to defend, no corporate power to invoke, no property to cherish, no ambition to pursue, bent beneath the fear of his masters, and the weight of a future without hope."

The arguments for and against a somewhat similar divorce of the peasant cultivator and stock-raiser from his native soil in Southern Africa are succinctly given by the late Maurice Evans :[1] "Many feel that the labour question will never be on a satisfactory basis while the native is thus rendered independent by having a home to which he can retire, and where, if he cannot live in affluence, he is able to satisfy his simple wants without feeling the pinch of necessity which forces the white man to industry. It is probable that in time to come, as the expansion and development of the country progress, the labour requirements will become more insistent, and the scarcity become more acutely felt. Aware that the one chief cause of the independence of the native is due to areas being reserved in which he can live his own life, without the necessity, ever present outside these areas, of

[1] In "Black and White in South East Africa."

having to labour for wages, agitation may be directed to the breaking up of the locations on the plea that it is demanded by the exigencies of the situation,[1] and, more plausibly, that it is in the real interests of the natives themselves that they should become steady workers instead of casual labourers, that only along this line lies their true development and permanent betterment. Already one hears the argument: The white man forced by his needs, must work twelve months in the year. A paternal Government does not provide him with land which gives him the opportunity to idle for half his time; and why should the native be placed in this position, retarding his own development and that of the country? Let the locations be broken up. For such remedy I hold we should pay too dearly. It may be that for a time labour would become more plentiful, and wages might fall, but a revolution in the habits[2] of a people, divorcing them from a life healthy and controlled, and transforming them into dwellers in uncongenial surroundings, would be to court disasters far greater than the inconvenience we now suffer. Already, the young people, the present generation, as I have

[1] In connection with such pleas of "exigencies" and "real interests" it is worthy of note that M. Renan has managed to put up a spirited defence for Ahab as against Naboth in the Bible history. He apparently wants us to regard Ahab "as a wise and progressive monarch, thwarted in a scheme of public improvement by those clerical anarchists, the prophets, and grossly libelled by the Tory High-Churchman who wrote that part of the Book of Kings."—See "My Neighbour's Landmark" [by Frederick Verinder].—A.S.C.

[2] Cf. "The Native's needs are fewer than ours, and his life less strenuous; but he is not inherently idle. Without clocks, factory bells, and taskmasters, he is accustomed to work for himself, his own way and time, and he is loth to leave his freedom, home, land and cattle for the sake of the slender rewards of the White man's service."—Willoughby: "Race Problems in the New Africa."—A.S.C.

pointed out, are being liberated from the salutary rules and customs which guarded the lives of their fathers, and the further emancipation which would necessarily follow such a violent change of life and environment would be disastrous, and probably result in our towns and industrial centres being overrun by a horde of vagabonds unrestrained by any ties or control excepting the law of the white man, not understood and unrecognized. What such a contact with ourselves as this would imply, though no one can predict its actual results, would in the main be maleficent."

Happily the question of what would be the actual results of a general break-up of the Native Reserves or Locations in South Africa has not been tested by actual experiment. But the effects of the Native Land Act, 1913, have supplied us with unpleasant demonstrations as to what those results would be. At a Conference on Native Affairs convened by the Dutch Reformed Church in the year 1923—" Chief Zibi showed how at present the one-sided administration of the Act had resulted in large numbers of natives wandering about with their families looking for places in which to live. Many had gone to swell the great army of native unemployed and many had become criminals in great towns."

Professor Brookes in his History of South Africa's Native Policy gives reasons why a movement of Natives to seek urban life is not to be desired. " Industrialists? It is neither for their good or ours that they should become industrialists permanently or on a large scale. They are far happier, far more moral, and in a far more natural state on the land than in the big towns,—that no one denies. The massing of Natives in centres like Witwatersrand—in spite of the Compound System, in spite of the fact that the Natives usually return to their homes in the Locations after their period of service, leads gradually to the growth of an Urban population, poor, squalid, propertyless, easily inflammable, whom the Bolshevik Third International has already designated the best material through which to spread communistic doctrine through Africa." He refers us to the Report of the Martial Law Judicial Commission, and goes on to say: "They are a prey for the agitator, interested, or disinterested, white or black, a potential menace to the community. Why make them unhappy in order to make ourselves unsafe? The only section profiting from the transaction is obviously big finance, usually absentee big finance, and therefore unafraid of the deluge."

I would urge that the ghost of a strangled protest from an England east-midland county be allowed at this point to speak on behalf of such South African pleadings as I have just cited—pleadings in stay of execution. Listen to the terms in which the petitioners of Raunds (Northants) begged long ago:

". . . leave to represent to the House that, under pretence of improving lands in the said parish, the cottagers and other persons entitled to rights of common on the lands intended to be enclosed, will be deprived of an inestimable privilege, which they now enjoy, of turning a certain number of their cows, calves, and sheep on and over the said lands . . . and they further conceive that a more ruinous effect of this enclosure will be the almost total depopulation of their town, now filled with bold and hardy husbandmen, from among whom, and the inhabitants of other open parishes, the nation has hitherto derived its greatest strength and glory in the supply of its fleets and armies, and driving them, from necessity and want of employ, in vast crowds, into manufacturing towns, where the very nature of their employment, over the loom or forge, soon may waste their strength, and consequently debilitate their posterity, and by imperceptible degrees obliterate that great principle of obedience to the laws of God and their country which forms the character of the simple artless villagers, more equally distributed through the open countries, and on which so much depends the good order and government of the State. . . ."

May the protest of "Black and White in South East Africa" succeed better than the Raunds petition succeeded! For it appears that the petitioners of this unfortunate Northamptonshire parish lost their rights to graze their stock on common lands and so to better their means of livelihood[1] owing to the passing of an Enclosure Act in 1797.

[1] Cf. what Tycho "the little god of small things" claims as well as warns in the Greek Anthology, "ask not for great things; since whatsoever a god of the commons can give to a labouring man, of this, I, Tycho, have control." "Select Epigrams" (Mackail's translation.)

CHAPTER IV

LAND-LUST AND OLIGARCHY

CHAPTER IV

["The men who pay wages ought not to be the political masters of those who earn them, because laws should be adapted to those who have the heaviest stake in the country, for whom misgovernment means not mortified pride, or stinted luxury, but want and pain and degradation and risk to their own lives and to their children's souls."—LORD ACTON.]

WE can see easily enough now, in this twentieth century, that the excuses made by our forefathers for plucking up by the roots England's old deeply-rooted rural life were insufficient. Nevertheless are not certain excuses recently made for tampering with Native African cultivation and pasturage, excuses for its dispossession and replacement, just as inadequate, and do they not fail in their attempt to carry conviction?

The Southern Rhodesian Native Reserves Commission made certain recommendations a few years ago, and to the bulk of the recommendations effect was given by an Order in Council, dated November 9th, 1920. It was a Commission imperially constituted, but its personnel was allowed to consist, without any exception whatsoever, of past or present British South Africa Company servants—at a time when the claim of that Company to all unalienated land in Southern Rhodesia had not as yet been disallowed.

An illuminating commentary on the activities of that Commission in the reduction of Native Reserve Acreage, on the favour with which those activities were regarded, and the self-congratulation which they awakened at the Chartered Company's Office in London, may be gathered from a speech that its Chairman, the impetuous Leander Starr Jameson, saw fit to make to its shareholders in the year 1917. He said:

" Now, gentlemen, besides that record of progress, in various directions measures have been taken to clear up ambiguities and uncertainties, to consolidate our position, and so make our property more valuable. Our native areas have always been in rather a fluid state. A Commission was appointed by the Imperial Government to enquire into the necessary areas to be set aside for the natives. Their report was finished, I think, at the beginning of last year. Since then it has been approved by the High Commissioner and the Imperial Government, and steps are now being taken to embody the result in a new Order in Council which will make that decision good for all time. The needs of the natives, both now and in the future, after careful examination by that Commission—which travelled all over the country, accompanied by our Surveyor-General—have been amply provided for, and the net result is that more than 1,000,000 acres of land have been added to the land which may be used for white settlement. That means really that you people get another 1,000,000 acres odd of what is called the unalienated land in the country. That is very satisfactory; but there is an unsatisfactory tag to it, and that is that at the present moment we have not got our clear title to the territory, because the title to all the unalienated land in the country is subject to the pending decision of the Privy Council. Well, we have done our utmost to hurry forward that decision, but the delays of lawyers are always proverbial, and when you get a Government added on to it, it seems interminable. Still, I am glad to say that counter-claims have been lodged, and our legal adviser, Mr. Coward, authorizes me to say that unless anything unforeseen should intervene the decision must be come to after the next Long Vacation—that is, we ought to have a decision before the end of the year. Of course, we are sure of the result."

It may be gathered that the Order in Council of 1920, embodying the bulk of this Commission's recommendations, amounted to the mulcting of the old Native Reserve Land as assigned in South Rhodesia, by a great number of acres, even allowing for the Commission's supposed charity of supererogation in placing certain back-blocks of country at the disposal of the tribes concerned. To quote the Commission, these back-blocks " will in fact be reserve reserves." How a Native population overflowing from free tribal land in their own more eligible localities can be regarded as receiving fairly equivalent compensation for eligible[1] Reserve land now expropriated, by the provision of free tribal land in the

[1] A scrap of evidence tendered to and printed by the Reserves Commission seems to be worthy of inclusion at this point : " R. Walsh, Manager of British South Africa Company's ranches, gave evidence as to existence of good ranching areas in certain Native Reserves."

Sebungwe District of sleeping-sickness renown, I find it difficult to understand.

It is not easy to condone the admittedly eclectic policy of this Reserves Commission (a point which I want to return to later on) as to seeking the testimony of the Natives themselves, nor is it easy to excuse its temerity in essaying to readjust the boundary of twenty million acres in a brief space of time (for the most part of it preoccupied war-time). Moreover I am not disposed to allow that the Commission's table of gains and losses (when comparing the old tentative Reserves acreage with the newly recommended Reserves demarcation) is a fair one. Reserves that were probably due to be provided sooner or later in more or less remote Districts[1] come for the first time into a published map of suggestions made under the auspices of this Reserves Commission. Thus they are allowed to pose as new benevolences, when they are really back debts of honour, left unpaid for about twenty years. Was it honest, *or was it dishonest*, to add in their acreage when the Table of Native Land Gains as against Losses was made up by this Reserves Commission of ours?

We have been assured that an imposing number of acres per head have been left for our Native population. But that assurance need not convince us that no harm has been done. Anyone who knows much of our granite veld, especially of certain Reserve tracts (e.g., a huge arid bush-veld tract in the Sabi Reserve) knows how little the imposing statement

[1] Wankie, Mtoko, and Gwanda Districts.

of this acreage is to be relied on in calculating how many human beings or cattle can be supported in a given area of it. Was not the standardized size of a European's farm for many years put at about 6,500 acres in Matabeleland, and in Mashonaland at about half that amount? When the Lemco Company took up their enormous holding at a very moderate rate indeed, were they not allowed a rebate even upon that price, barren rock being roughly estimated for, and omitted from the reckoning?

Part of the land of Palestine was not unlike part of Mashonaland, I should imagine, but Josephus tells us of Joshua that he "thought the land for the tribes should be divided by estimation of its goodness, rather than the largeness of its measure, it often happening that one acre of some sort of land was equivalent to a thousand other acres." At a time when the tenure of so many Natives in Europeans' lands as rent-paying tenants was so precarious, a time when both the Native was apparently so fast increasing and Native agriculture so fast developing, it was not easy to agree to great tracts of Mashonaland being lost to Native tribal occupation with any sort of notion that it was all for the best.

It seems deplorable that in Southern Rhodesia and Kenya[1] alike, subject races had their tribal acreage mulcted soon after the War, when they had given in the War-time such proofs of loyalty.

[1] The East Africa Report tells us that the local Governor, Sir E. Northey, confiscated some of the land of the Nandi tribe, which had helped us in the war, for a soldiers' settlement, and delayed to tell the Colonial Office what he had done.

If, generally speaking, the West African has often had reason to bless our Imperial Government's fostering care in the course of the last few decades, has not the African of the South or of the East often had occasion to curse our exploitations in the same period? Has he not time and time again "looked for judgment, but behold oppression; for righteousness, but behold a cry"?

I do not think that Maurice Evans was writing as a mere alarmist when he denounced the curse of land-hunger in South Africa a few years back: we have seen what we have seen since he wrote:

"Land-hunger, which exists everywhere, but which is a special feature of new countries, is prevalent in South Africa. One after another, native territories have been taken, and now longing eyes are cast on Basutoland and Swaziland, and many express a desire that these countries should be opened up. I trust the sense of justice of South Africa will over-rule the greed of those who would strip the native of the little he has left."[1]

Should the question that was decided in October, 1922 (by Referendum) of Southern Rhodesia, with its hundreds of thousands of Africans, being absorbed

[1] Compare what Sir F. Benson said in an article in "Outward Bound"—"Part of the inevitable problem of Rhodesia and the 'native reserves.'" He has been showing how in Shakespeare's "The Tempest," Caliban complains that he was made much of by Prospero when Prospero first came to the island, and had proved his own usefulness to him, showing him "all the qualities of the isle. . . ." But, according to Caliban, Prospero the immigrant has proved a tyrant to the isle's inhabitant whom he found there when he landed. Caliban says:

> ". . . here you sty me
> On this hard rock, while you do keep from me
> The rest o' the island."

in South Africa's Union, arise once more, let the Imperial Government remember these words. The great Oligarchy of the Union Dominion, with its hankerings for secession, and its exaggerated view of Dominion Status, must not be allowed to absorb these loyal S. Rhodesian Natives without definite Imperial Guarantees of a reasonable type.

Let the British Government remember, too, how the Parable of the Rich Man's petition to Father Abraham that he should send to warn brethren, not in the place of torment yet, lest they should come into it, was recalled by a Native spokesman in the Union, when the question trembled in the balance. "This place of torment!" It is significant indeed, as a description of our great South African Dominion wherein European Dives with his Land-Lust and African Lazarus with his Land-Hunger co-exist as contemporaries.

It has been urged, and rightly, as it seems to me, that Christ apparently felt more concern for the soul of Dives than for the sores of Lazarus in the propounding of His searching parable. Nevertheless, His teaching was, I take it, that the soul of Dives was intimately affected by his care or neglect of Lazarus' sores. The wrongs of the dispossessed and disinherited in those English villages of three generations ago did much harm, doubtless, to those that dispossessed them, the powers-that-were of a brilliant era.[1] In "The Sabi Reserve" (published by Black-

[1] Mr. Gilbert Chesterton's memorable phrase about the village green, that had got mislaid, turning up in the squire's back-yard, tells us concisely some of the outstanding truth about that brilliant era.

well, Oxford, in 1920) the present writer was able to give some idea of how the fever of dispossession was affecting, at that time, one particular District (the Charter District in which I lived) in Mashonaland. I wrote that there was every reason to believe that perhaps 200 more tribesfolk (or, say 1,000 souls) would have to leave private lands in the course of a year or two. In ten years' time we might have to face a situation of practically no more Natives being left in ordinary alienated lands,[1] so that possibly a population of 7,000 to 8,000 might soon be perforce moving.

It is of our Karana (Mashona)[2] tribes that Sir H. H. Johnston has written :

" They are dogged, industrious, and patient agriculturists, enormously attached to the soil, whereon they and their ancestors have dwelt for a period we may guess at being unusually long for Bantu history." (" The Black Man's Part in the War.")

A liberal policy in general (and that must include a generous land settlement in particular) towards the Native peasant population in South Africa means a clear moral gain to that alien oligarchy which rules

[1] An ex-Native Commissioner, Mr. Alfred Drew, in a Paper read to a South Rhodesian Conference in 1924, said : " In the wilds of the country isn't it better for the natives to be saving a farm from becoming a wilderness, than for them to be sent into a reserve ? Another aspect of the matter is that in some parts of the country the reserves are said to be small and congested, and we shall hear less about this if the natives are not hurried off places which they prefer to the reserves. . . ." The recommendation of our Lands Commission (dealt with at the end of this volume) with regard to removing Natives with a rent-paying agreement from private lands of Europeans requires grave consideration.

[2] Various tribes are grouped together under the Mashona name or nickname, e.g., in the Charter District there are Wahera, Wanjanja, Warozwi, Waromo, etc.

them. To quote our South African prophet (of land-reform)'s pregnant saying once again about the psychological effect which may follow hard upon the adoption of such a policy.—" For the white man it will mean much to his inner life."

In Southern Rhodesia at least, where so much land, as yet unalienated, has been transferred by the Imperial Government to our might-be Commonwealth's disposal, the question of the land-settlement of two teachable and adaptive Native Nations with their passions for ploughing or stock-raising is still in a plastic stage, as I hope to make clear in this volume.

My Mashona friends' material future (marriage to their own veld-soil, or partial divorce from it owing to the absence of ample and acceptable Native Areas) looks to be as clay in our responsibly (or irresponsibly) governing hands. Have we, who, for all our flaunted democratic principles at home, are apt to be oligarchs overseas, a mind to treat these Africans as our English oligarchy[1] treated English country labourers in the days of their votelessness ? Let us try to see dispossession, by the light of our own English history, as what it is—a lure, a blind, a curse to our Imperial Commonwealth ! Let us awake to the fact that a million Rhodesian Acres go a very small way in the provision of huge cattle-ranching estates for European colonists, but go a very great way in the provision of room-to-plough for African peasants.

[1] An advertisement in an English paper (May, 1924) which concerns the Cape Province in South Africa, attractively advises the taking of " THE DIRECT ROUTE TO THE LIFE OF A COUNTRY SQUIRE."

CHAPTER V

THE HOPE OF A TRUSTEESHIP POLICY

CHAPTER V

[" . . . I believe the desire for a change of heart is a genuine longing, and, furthermore, I believe firmly that unless the World Order is affected by this change of heart, the World Order is doomed. . . . Unless it can keep its rule over subject peoples quite free from the spirit of commercial exploitation and the spirit of slavery, and make it like the rule of a good citizen over his fellows, it will be shattered by the widespread hatred of those whom it rules."
—PROFESSOR GILBERT MURRAY, " Essays and Addresses."]

NOT without reason in July, 1921, might a representative member of the Northern Rhodesian Settlers' Advisory Council prelude his confession of faith in a policy of trusteeship towards Native Africans by a notable admission : " The actual policy in vogue to-day (so far as there was a policy) was one of exploitation, tempered by more or less sympathetic administration." Have not the old reasons that were to blame in the England of a century ago, been to blame far too often in the Africa of our own day—I mean the joining of house to house, the laying of field to field ? " No career," to quote that alluring announcement of South African farming prospects I quoted before, " is more absorbing than planning and evolving, as through the centuries so many in Britain have done, a landed estate for one's family."

Lord Olivier's words about the relations of Master

and Man in the Tropics have a distinct bearing on those relations as we find them in semi-tropical Southern Rhodesia or parts of Africa with a still more temperate climate.—" No one can raise any question whatsoever that the policy of the development through large estates, involves, if it is to succeed, the expropriation of natives, not only because the grantees want themselves to have land and its produce, but because they want the natives to have none, in order that the natives may be forced to work for them." So much for the policy of large estates.

" The Village Labourer"[1] unfolds the iniquities of a widespread change in land tenure, a change effected over the heads of those politically inarticulate commoners, who stood to lose by it. British notions of political fair play have surely grown in sensitiveness since the days of the French War's enclosures, and in the recent Great War's experiences have made a really significant advance. In a notable preface to his compilation on Indian reform, Mr. Lionel Curtis has told us :

" To insist that the war has done nothing to open our eyes or stimulate our energies is sheer blindness. It compelled England, as nothing else could have done, to recognize that the principles for which she was fighting could not be restricted to the peoples of Europe, America and Australia, but must be extended to those of Asia and Africa."

In the light of those really fine words how does our twentieth century treatment of the African land

[1] J. L. and B. Hammond's standard historical treatise.

question alike in the Union, and in Southern Rhodesia, appear ?

It was represented by the South African Native Affairs Commission of 1903-5 that the time for finality had come in the provision of land for Native Occupation. The Reserves Commission of Southern Rhodesia, whose personnel and recommendations we have already had occasion to refer to, was commissioned to make a final assignation of Southern Rhodesian Native Reserve lands in accordance with this view. But how could a satisfactory final settlement in the Union as to that Union's Land Act be reached? For we read in "The Evolution of South African Native Policy" (J. Y. Gibson, 1919, page 55): "There was no suggestion that the Natives might be consulted." Earl Buxton, High Commissioner in the Union of South Africa from 1914-1920, says of what he calls "the very delicate and troublesome problem of Territorial Segregation—that is the land delimitation of the White and Black Races"—"This difficult problem can be dealt with better . . . when the Natives can be consulted as well as the Europeans."

Sir William Beaumont, President of that Beaumont Commission which essayed to recommend complementary Native Areas to those already scheduled in connection with the Union Land, has made a declaration to this effect :

"If the defined (already) Native areas are examined, it will be found that most of them are already largely occupied by Natives, and that there is not much room for more, while in some areas the lands are so poor or so malarial, or so distant that the Natives would not go to them."

How can the award made by Order in Council as to Southern Rhodesian Native Reserve acreage be regarded as aught but an augmentable minimum? For we have that Commission's own admission as to how meagrely they consulted the Natives in those deliberations of theirs on which the award was mainly based. What they said in substance was this :

"We did not, as a rule, examine native chiefs unless there was some point to be elucidated or some definite information to be gained. In many reserves it was not possible, for various reasons, to consider any alteration of boundary, and in some other cases the direction which our recommendations must take was so obvious that the local chiefs were not examined. We felt that we might do more harm than good by questioning the Natives upon a matter of which they were very likely to misunderstand the real scope, and to which also no effect could be given for a year or more."

After such an admission made, the claim to make this recent settlement of all lands to be held by Native tribes of Southern Rhodesia a final[1] settlement is arguably premature. One is thankful that an irreducible minimum of Native Reserve lands has been placed as an Imperial Trust for Natives in the hands

[1] It has not been, I am thankful to say, treated as such. Certain augmentations have already been given effect to, being "set aside by notice issued by the Governor in Council for the occupation and use of Natives." The Land Commission's Report (dated 1925), records, and recommends as to, these augmentations in its paragraph 143.

of Britain's High Commissioner. But taking up my stand on Britain's now recognized principle of self-determinism I refuse to consider this Trust as an unaugmentable maximum, as long as our Natives are, as now, politically inarticulate. Should Advisory Councils of Natives be constituted in Mashonaland and Matabeleland, a step would be taken towards the securing of that Native representative opinion which has never yet been either invited or obtained satisfactorily.

Well might *The Field* draw marked attention to that pronouncement made in the Settlers' Advisory Council of Northern Rhodesia (July, 1921), which I have quoted already.

It explained to us that, coming from such a source, the views enunciated were somewhat unexpected, but were all the more welcome as an indication that leading men among the settlers in British Central Africa were alive to the needs of the time. It went on to say that this memorandum dealt with one of the really big questions affecting the future of Africa, " though hitherto those calling attention to the issues it defines have been as voices crying in the wilderness. The Advisory Council of Settlers for Northern Rhodesia cannot be dismissed as cranks and fanatics. . . ."

What those views were as to the Natives and their Land Question I find recorded concisely in a " summary of the proposals printed by *The Times* of October 7th, 1921 :

" LAND.—Immediate steps to remove Native apprehensions as to security of tenure. The native must be convinced that he was secured for ever in possession of sufficient land suitable for his probable development."

I would pass on from that triumphant general statement of a sound principle as to Natives and Land, which was coined in Northern Rhodesia, to some particular statements made by a high authority as to the Natives and Land position in Southern Rhodesia, that part of Africa with which I have been in touch for over twenty-five years, and which is the main concern of my volume. I wish to quote our Chief Native Commissioner as to the development of our Natives. In one of his recent Annual Reports he told us :

" An active class of small farmers is being evolved, which augurs well for the Native's future, and is a development which deserves every encouragement. The natives of this country no longer form a source of supply of purely unskilled labour: they are producers with increasing productive possibilities."

Again the same authority says :

" The Reserves will for a long time uphold tribalism, which, though being modified by the advance of civilization cannot be supplanted in the present stage of native development. . . . The natives will dissociate themselves from tribalism as they become fitted by character, education, and intelligence to stand alone. The tribal system will thus gradually disappear, but no sudden breaking down of such system should be attempted."

Yet he sees that the road should be kept open for the African's own self-determination as to the adoption of another form of land-tenure.

" In my last report I again advocated the reservation of land for acquisition by Natives. The matter is still under consideration. In the interests of all alike it is not desirable that natives should acquire land indiscriminately, owing to the inevitable friction which will arise with their European neighbours. It is advisable, therefore, to reserve land contiguous to existing reserves for individual purchase or lease by them. The question is one which requires careful consideration, but an early solution; for delay will increase the difficulties of carrying any such scheme into effect. Land is a basis of national wealth. The aspirations of the Natives to a portion of it on terms which secure individual title are legitimate. Any attempt to restrict a people from seeking an outlet for its potential development in that direction is foolish."

As to another need of African land for Africans, that has arisen with the growth of a native industrial population living in locations with little or no garden ground to cultivate, the same authority has something to say that is well worth hearing :

" A large percentage of the Natives employed in the townships are married, and live with their wives and families. These form a steady supply of labour. The conditions of life in the average location offer few attractions to any Native with well-regulated habits, and are inimical to domestic and family welfare. . . . It is a pleasure to record that Salisbury Municipal Council has taken the initiative by surveying plots of land for leasing to married natives employed in the town. It is earnestly to be hoped that this wise step will be followed by other municipal bodies in the country."

That the Policy of Trusteeship has brought new hope into the Native Question in Southern Rhodesia scarcely requires the further proof that these stirring and utterly unequivocal words of Sir John Chancellor[1] to the Agricultural Union of the Colony he governs, contain :

"A fundamental principle of the British Empire is that everybody enjoys freedom under the British flag. Every subject of the King is free to enter into a contract or to abstain from entering into a contract for the disposal of his labour. Any measures taken by Government to apply compulsion to natives to secure an adequate supply of labour for private employers would be opposed to the traditional policy of His Majesty's Government, and would be altogether repugnant to the sentiment of the Imperial Parliament.[2] Any agitation to secure the introduction of compulsory labour would react unfavourably upon the reputation of Rhodesia. . . ."

But is any application of the Doctrine of Trusteeship however sound, likely to afford present help in the

[1] First Governor of H.M. Colony of S. Rhodesia (appointed in 1923).

[2] Sir John Chancellor spoke these plain words in 1925. Recently an agitation to oust the Imperial Government from that supreme control of Native Affairs which it possesses in Southern Rhodesia, has excited some little attention. A letter printed in *The Rhodesian Herald* for Christmas Eve, 1926, deserves quotation here as giving the case for Imperial Government control in a very few words :

"What, apparently, a small section of the European community desires is the 'entire control of the natives,' so that they may be exploited in its own interests without fear of outside interference. The Native is to have no rights except such as his white masters are graciously pleased to concede. Their will is to be his law. The justice given him must only be such as does not conflict with their own interests! And this in a sports-loving British Colony!

"Even in sport, where both sides are animated by the same sports-

trouble that Mr. Peter Nielsen has indicated in the treatise we have already drawn upon? He tells us the simple truth about this trouble:

"The hardships and disabilities under which the educated Native suffers in the Northern Provinces of the Union and in Rhodesia are patent and serious. It is hard that a civilized man may not travel in his own country without a "certificate"; it is hard that he must do only rough or menial, but always ill-paid work when he is capable of doing skilled and well-paid labour; it is hard that when he is allowed to do skilled labour he cannot claim the wages of a skilled labourer; it is hard to be denied always the privileges of a civilized existence for which he has proved himself fit and worthy; it is hard to be treated always as an inferior and an alien in the land of his fathers; all this is hard, but—'tis the law, written and unwritten, made and enforced by the dominant race, and there is no reason to think it will be made less hard, as the pressure of black competition increases."

For this dark and uneasy state of affairs Mr. Nielsen, who stands for Native self-development, has but the one suggestion by way of general remedy. What that suggestion is we must now pass on to consider.

manlike spirit and where there is nothing at stake except 'kudos,' an umpire is necessary. Either side would rather forfeit the game than secure an unfair advantage, but the player is not in a position to see all that happens; he is 'on the spot.' Only the man who is not playing, and is not concerned further with the verdict than that it should be impartial, can really judge.

"In the great tussle between black and white there is, I am convinced, a real desire to give the other side a fair show. But here the issues are tremendous. It is literally a struggle for existence. More than ever do we need the unbiased referee here."

CHAPTER VI

THE HOPE OF A TERRITORIAL SEGREGATION POLICY

CHAPTER VI

[" The land question means hunger, thirst, nakedness, notice to quit, labour spent in vain, the toil of years seized upon, the breaking up of homes; the misery of parents, children and wives; the despair and wildness that springs up in the hearts of the poor when legal force like a sharp arrow, goes over the most sensitive and vital rights of mankind. All this is concerned in the land question."—CARDINAL MANNING.]

I DESIRE to associate myself with Mr. Nielsen in his view that, things being what they are in our Anglo-Dutch part of the British Empire, " the policy of territorial separation is the only policy that will make possible a home existence for the Natives in their own homeland, for we know that however educated and however worthy the civilized Native may become, he cannot hope to find a home, or to feel at home among the whites. . . .

" But in their own areas the Natives will have their own homes and their own home-life, without which human existence is indeed miserable. Those among them who long for the privilege of private ownership will be able to acquire land in freehold in localities set aside therefor, while those who cling to the old ways will be allowed to continue as before under their old system of communal land-tenure."

I believe that they managed civic matters in some respects far better in the old Roman Empire, and are managing things far better in the modern French Empire. Yet, the soul-rotting prejudices encouraged by the servile atmosphere of Black-and-White life in South African Mixed Areas being what I know them to be, I incline towards that comparatively equitable compromise which Mr. Nielsen, following the late Maurice Evans, preaches :

" But if good and ample land can be set aside in the various territories of spacious South Africa in which the Natives can live and move without let or hindrance; in which they can do what work they like for themselves and for their own people; in which they can engage according to their individual desires, in all kinds of trade and commerce without the prohibitions of the white man's colour-bar; in which they can earn the wages that are governed by the laws of supply and demand only; in which they can build up after their own fashion courts of law and political councils for themselves; in which, in fine, they can live and work out their own salvation, unhurried and unworried by strange and impatient masters, then, surely the Natives of South Africa will have gained a great gain far greater than any they can ever hope to win by putting their undeveloped strength[1] against the organized resistance of the whites."

[1] Cf. the sardonic remark of Sir Charles Eliot about that East African Native Protectorate he was supposed to be protecting : " Your Lordship has opened this Protectorate to white immigration and colonization, and I think it well that, in confidential correspondence at least, we should face the undoubted issue, viz., that white mates black in a very few moves."—A.S.C.

Self-determination and self-development are surely required by our Natives, and how are they to attain to a proper measure of either—conditions and feeling in South Africa being what one has found them to be by long experience? Self-development and self-determination need to be stressed in my opinion if we are to seek any really hopeful settlement of the Native question in our Colony.

The able Rhodesian writer I have quoted, arguing with long experience and detailed observation as his allies, assures us that the Bantu ought to be given a better field for self-development than they now have afforded them, and one exempt from such excessive European interference as harasses them to-day.

"The Native," he tells us, "is not a savage." He is meant then doubtless by Providence to fulfil a racial destiny of his own, not that career of mere serf or parasite, which is too often allotted to him in South Africa.

Good indeed is it for us British Imperialists to be reminded, as Mr. Nielsen reminds us, of a certain saying coined by our Roman forerunners: "As many slaves so many enemies."

The memorable words of Sir Henry Campbell-Bannerman spoken in relation to another Racial Question in South Africa are obviously applicable to the Native Question that is present with us in His Majesty's new-born Colony of Southern Rhodesia: "Good government can never be a satisfactory substitute for self-government."

The benefits of a Segregation Policy based on a fair

dividing up of Land Areas (a dividing-up which appears to be far more easily attainable at the present time in Southern Rhodesia than in the Union of South Africa) have been expounded by the present Prime Minister of that Union, General Hertzog :

" I want to remind you that the Native Policy of to-day, the policy which is followed this moment and will be followed in its further development, is to secure the Native in his own territory, every possible scope of employment for him, and the white man shall not be allowed in to oust him from those territories. After all it is not asking much. When it concerns the white, we take the power to see, if the occasion requires it, that the native shall understand he is within the white man's territory, and he must give him a chance. I do not want to go further into this. The policy of the Government is—and I have always insisted on this and I insist upon it to-day as strongly as ever—that what we allow to ourselves we shall allow to the Native, and what we allow to Natives we must allow to ourselves."

In that compendious hand-book to General Hertzog's Policy of Segregation and Differentiation, his " History of Native Policy in South Africa," Professor Brookes advances some considerations that commend this Policy as a temporary expedient to Philo-Africans, who know present-day South African feeling and conditions, however completely they refuse and detest some of the pseudo-ideals of such a Policy.

" We must make it our aim, then, to preserve the

independent existence of a pure[1] white race, embracing all social classes in South Africa—but every one of the arguments for preserving the individuality of the white race is an argument also for preserving the individuality of the black. We may mould and direct their energies as we will, but we may not place bars across their upward path. . . . When we think of Mazzini's grand conception of every nation having its 'mission' to humanity, which no one else can fulfil, we cannot but think that the vast group of negro and Bantu races also have their contribution to make to the unseen universe of thought in which we live. . . .

"To divert Native aspirations into the path of differential development is possible: thereby white and black individuality will both benefit. But to hold all Natives down in a position of permanent inferiority will ultimately beget a deep and bitter race hatred which will aim, not at the autonomy of the black but at the extermination of the white, if once a huge war of extermination between white and black broke out in South Africa, it is idle to argue that the white would win. He would, of course, with his machine guns and aeroplanes and other 'civilized' devices, but it would be a Pyrrhic victory. It is not merely of the tens of thousands of white men, women and

[1] But the Rev. W. A. Cotton, C.R., is quite right in confronting "South Africa with the fact that during four hundred years Europeans *as a race*, the Nordic elements as unquestionably as the Alpine and Mediterranean, have continuously lacked, and confessedly do still lack, the gift of continence in their relations with the coloured peoples whom they have brought under their sway." I agree with him also when he goes on to say: "Consequently the prohibition of marriages is very gravely to be reprobated. The remedy for this sin must be made available." "The Race Problem in South Africa" [S.C.M.]—A.S.C.

children who would be massacred that one thinks. It is rather of the brutalized and demoralized condition that the cruelties and barbarities of a long war of extermination would produce in the scanty remnants of the white race which survived it.

" 'Survivors,' as Tacitus puts it, 'not only of the others but of themselves.'

" The policy of identity would produce deep-seated hatred of the black man by the white. The policy of subordination would produce deep-seated hatred of the white man by the black. There is only one way out—a way narrow indeed, unexplored, dangerous and difficult, but safer than the raging torrents and tremendous precipices to right and left—the path of differential development, the course dictated by that true liberalism, which has ever stood for the preservation of small nationalities, the course dictated by that wise conservatism which is not prepared to sacrifice national institutions and natural divisions for an unknown and fear-inspiring future. For the preservation and happiness of white and black alike, we stand for the policy of differentiation."

Such for good and for evil is this Policy, which some of us are welcoming as offering the Native Races a chance such as they are not now getting of living their own lives as men, and not as serfs or parasites, and bringing to fruition what is so admirable and distinctive in their own immemorial race characterization.

" Regarding the Natives of Rhodesia," says Mr. Nielsen, " I am able to say that all the elderly Native men with whom I have spoken about this subject—and I have conversed with a large number—agree that the policy as outlined in the Native Lands Act and the Native Affairs Act of 1920, as I have explained it to them, is good and sound. . . .

"The protests that have been made from the Native side, moreover, have been directed against the hardship caused through harshness in carrying out the Act in certain places, and against the relative smallness of the areas[1] proposed for Native occupation, and not against the principle itself. . . ."

In stating that Natives in the Charter District of Mashonaland, which has been my home for many years, desire Segregation Areas (away from Europeans' Farms and Estates) I do not think my statement is likely to be seriously questioned. In May, 1925, a Lands Commission, which has been appointed to consider the question of Territorial Segregation in our Colony, took evidence in that District. The evidence of Paramount Chief Maromo and other Native witnesses given on that occasion may be found to

[1] As to that veritable mountain of difficulty, the provision of equitable Native Areas in accordance with any consistent Territorial Segregation Policy in the Union of South Africa, General Hertzog has spoken out with the ring of faith in his utterance (I quote *The South African Outlook* for August, 1925): "I admit that your Native has not been satisfactorily dealt with up to now. When that law was accepted in 1913 it was said to the Natives, 'We are going to give you more than we have assigned to you in these schedules.' I am fully determined we are going to comply with what we held out to the Natives at that time. It is going to be part of my endeavour to put the Native question on a proper footing, and see that he gets what was promised him in 1913 as far as the land is concerned." But the recently proposed land legislation in the Union of S. Africa cannot be regarded as satisfactorily fulfilling this chivalrous undertaking. The criticism issued by a Joint Council of Europeans and Natives for promoting Native welfare in Johannesburg on General Hertzog's Natives and Land Policy proposals is worthy of most serious attention.—A.S.C.

support my argument that Native opinion itself demands the provision of Territorial Areas as a means to further Native Self-Determinism and Native Self-Development.

I commend the Natives' own desire for Segregation Areas in the South African Colony I am dealing with as the most important human argument in favour of them.

The position of our Natives encouraged to plunge into the new go-ahead life of the Southern Rhodesia Colony, but denied a place in the sun as regards that self-development on the soil which really appeals to them, while the arts of cajolery are used to induce more and more Europeans to acquire vested rights on easy terms in that soil appeals to me as pathetic and ominous of tragedy. Oh, the pity of it ![1]

[1] DRUM-BEATS IN SOUTHERN RHODESIA

(*See Jeremiah xxii for this Music of the Drums*).

Hear the Lords of our land
    Hailing their kith and their kin
(Strangers and aliens all !)—
    " Come ye, and enter ye in !
Come ye, add farm unto farm !
    Come ye, for yet there is room ! "
We that were born in our land
    Hear them, and brood in our gloom.
    O Earth, Earth, Earth,
    Hear the Word of the Lord !

Cramp'd in our close-lopp'd land-leavings
    Hear we, and Faith from us flees :
Dry breasts and wombs that miscarry—
    Where is our Hope but in these ?
Ploughs they have sold for our ploughing :
    Will they sell us earth with a plough ?
Their bulls, for our herds we have bought them :
    Will they haggle o'er grass for them now ?
    O Earth, Earth, Earth,
    Hear the Word of the Lord !

'Tis Shame, Shame, Shame—
    They grudge to men their mother—
EARTH, EARTH, EARTH, EARTH—
    MOTHER EARTH, my brother!
Mercies in snares they have taken:
    Rights in their pitfalls are dead:
Let them hear in the thud of our drum-beats
    Jehovah's thunders and dread!
    O Earth, Earth, Earth,
    Hear the Word of the Lord!

CHAPTER VII

DAYBREAK FOR DARKNESS

CHAPTER VII

> " Like day she came
> Making the night a dream."
> —P. B. Shelley

> " Certain men slept upon a plain, and the night was chill and dark. And, as they slept, at that hour when night is darkest, one stirred. Far off to the eastward, through his half-closed eyelids, he saw, as it were, one faint line, thin as a hair's width, that edged the hill tops. And he whispered in the darkness to his fellows : ' The dawn is coming.' But they, with fast-closed eyelids murmured, ' He lies, there is no dawn.' Nevertheless, day broke."
> —Olive Schreiner.

NOT contemptuously or callously, but from true love for Africa and Africans, and with tried faith in her and in them, the writer of these words owns to cherishing a daybreak hope in Territorial Segregation, writing as he does when one dark hour succeeds another, and each dark hour is apt to seem somewhat darker than the last.

In September, 1923, the subject of " *Segregation as a fundamental plank in Native Policy* " secured attention at a Johannesburg Conference on Native Affairs. Various reasons were given there in support of the drastic view that " Complete Segregation was a policy wholly impracticable of fulfilment." On the other hand it would appear to have been admitted there that "Partial Segregation was a very different matter: quite possible of fulfilment, and much to be desired." In the course of Professor Macmillan's lecture delivered to the same Conference, cordial if tardy amends were rendered to a much abused pioneer Missionary of a former generation, Dr. Philip. "Alone in his day, he saw that the native problem was a land problem, and alone among his contemporaries he advocated a policy of separate areas."

The present writer sees in the policy of providing ample and acceptable separated Native Areas some real, if rather dim hope[1] of daybreak for Native African Life in Anglo-Africa. His own passionate conviction is that this life has much in it clearly meriting as well as rightfully claiming liberty for self-development, and that such liberty may be fostered and extended by a measure of Territorial Segregation. Stones instead of bread have been doled out far too often to their Native families by paternal Anglo-African Governments. In relief of that indigence of opportunity which stunts the present life of Native Anglo-Africa, one would welcome Segregation, even in a much modified form, if it were to mean the provision of ample and acceptable Native Areas.

[1] Mr. Nielsen warns us quite sensibly not to expect too much of a Native Areas Policy. "No reasonable person will expect that this policy will do away entirely with all the little troubles that arise from the clashing of opposite racial interests. In the white areas the Native who can come there only as a labourer or visitor, not as a settler, will remain a subordinate to the whites. . . . But if tolerance and honesty prevail in our councils we shall be able to adjust and settle the many questions that are bound to arise from time to time."—"The Black Man's Place in South Africa."

For the partial benefaction of half a loaf is better than no bread for the hungry.

Where is the reasoned case for a policy of segregation to be found in a compact form? Two books may be named, the two I have already used so often to shape my own argument. One is that compendious Natal treatise published more than half a generation ago now—"Black and White in South-East Africa" (Longmans & Co.). That book argues in a leisurely, well-considered and all-round fashion of its own, a generous agrarian policy as due on the part of the ruling European race to the subject African races inhabiting Anglo-Africa—a policy "making the black man's land attractive to him, freeing him from the irritation and overlordship of individual whites and giving him every opportunity for personal and race development."

The other book is that brief Rhodesian treatise published by Messrs. Juta of Cape Town much more recently. In it, as we have seen, Mr. Nielsen, its author, grapples with the task of showing good reason for accepting with confidence "the Bantu as the equals of Europeans in every respect save past achievement." Moreover in it the aforesaid author goes on to face the apparent verdict of recent Anglo-African History that "the whites and the blacks cannot live in peace and goodwill together in one place", and contends "that territorial separation is the only way to lasting peace and happiness in South Africa."

It seems to me that the second of these two books, which I have named, the Rhodesian one, supplies just such reinforcement as the Natal book has long required, if some entrenchments of Anglo-Dutch South African prejudice, which the accretions and entanglements of generations have made formidable, are to be carried, and the frontal attack of Higher (or Christian) Imperialism pressed home. The Natal book had shown reasonable cause for belief that the South African Native Question was largely a Land Question, and that a liberal Land Policy for Natives had every sound civic argument on its side. But somehow South Africa has, generally speaking, refused as yet any general movement of conversion from repressionist and exploitationist errors—any such movement as might have found expression in acts of eager amendment and generous reparation planned to benefit those who were proved to have had less than justice. Why?

I think that a true answer may be found in the fact that though South Africa has to some extent felt the appeal and driving force of the arguments adduced, she has all the time been to a greater, or less, extent haunted by one persistent obsession, already referred to in Chapter II: I mean the obsession that men of the Native Race in Africa are something less than men[1]; and that pleas based on human rights and

[1] In the Report of the late Maurice Evans on certain Native Areas in Natal and Zululand (which had been recommended by a Natives Land Commission) we read: "The Europeans particularly objected to any good land being included in the recommended Native areas. The fact that any portion of the recommended areas was good either for agricultural or pastoral purposes was advanced by them as a sufficient argument for its exclusion." Moreover, we are given by Mr. Evans this significant anecdote: "At the meeting the Nondweni farmers (whose farms are not included in native areas) urged that

sympathies fail somehow to carry conviction where Natives are concerned. This is surely where the usefulness of "The Black Man's Part in South Africa" may come in. Mr. Peter Nielsen, as we have seen, has set himself to ask and to answer that recurrent question: "Is the African Native equal to the European in mental and moral capacity, or is he not?" The interrogator's scientific studies and his practical experience of Natives combine together in helping him to find the reply to his own question. He answers it in the Native's favour. Before he has done with us he has given us reasonable proofs of the essential humanity of those Races to which the White Races in South Africa quite evidently owe so much by way of delayed Reparations instalments. After admitting that Machiavelli's dark view of human nature seems to him as applicable to the black man of South Africa as to those white men whom Machiavelli had in mind, Mr. Nielsen quotes Shakespeare's "What a piece of work is man! How noble in reason! How infinite in faculty!" as expressing "the wonder I have often felt at the wealth of imagery, the mental grasp, the wisdom and the natural dignity in very many untutored natives I have met with, and it is that experience which makes me believe that the present difference between the European and the Native race is one of degree, and not of kind, and that, in the fullness of time, achievement will follow the

their land be taken into native area on an exchange basis. They represented that on account of the poorness of the soil it was only fit for natives." (Blue Book, U.G. 41, 1918.)

latent genius with which, as I hold, Nature has endowed in equal degree with ourselves the great Bantu branch of the human family." After this manner the later (Rhodesian) book acts as a complement to the earlier (Natal) book, and prepares a likely way for the acceptance of that very able book's conclusions.

But you may say, "What about the case against Segregation?" A case against Segregation, at variance with the converging arguments proffered in such profusion by those two books which I have cited, can be studied clearly and concisely in a letter printed by *The Friend* newspaper of Bloemfontein in October, 1923. Dr. Schalkwyck, of Graaff-Reinet, wrote as follows: "By segregating the Native you remove all the factors which tend to diminish his natural increase —excess of births over deaths. By reverting to his former mode of life, and by discarding European habits and customs the struggle for existence for him will become less. Polygamy will flourish again with resultant large families. He will be away from European diseases and strong drink.[1] Moreover, the national sentiment will be revived and fostered, and the native will become a menace to the white man. Keep him dispersed among the whites, and he cannot organize. Keep him in touch with the Europeans and his natural increase will diminish. In many towns the death-rate of the non-European is only slightly less than the birth-rate, and is, in any case,

[1] A member of the Southern Rhodesian Legislative Assembly in the session of 1925 took the line that the Native was being given an unfair advantage by being prohibited from obtaining European liquor. —A.S.C.

from two to five times higher than the European death-rate. It is an indisputable fact that the more the native adopts methods and customs of civilization the greater will be his struggle for existence and the more his natural increase will diminish."

How successfully the Policy of Mixed Areas in the Union of South Africa has kept the mortality of urban Natives a high one! A lecturer in Salisbury, Mashonaland (July, 1922),[1] dealing with the question of race contact, gave some information about Native life (or death) in the Union of South Africa's town areas: "East London was one of the few towns where vital statistics had been kept, and there they found that the infantile mortality among native children born in that area was 450 per 1,000. That meant that nine out of every twenty children died before they were one year old. . . .

"The Kimberley location was horrible, and the Johannesburg one was a dreadful spot in most of its aspects. Bloemfontein was a bright spot. . . .

"In the Union they had some of the worst conditions at Kimberley and Johannesburg,[2] and of the best at Bloemfontein and Durban."

Such an outspoken attack as that which Dr. Schalkwyck has made on a Segregation Policy may surely

[1] The reference is to a lecture by that able Philo-African, Dr. C. T. Loram of the Union Native Affairs Commission.

[2] In the Preface to Mr. W. C. Scully's "Daniel Varenna," which is dated 1922, the Bantu population in and around Johannesburg is stated to average more than 200,000, more than nine-tenths of whom are males. The same Preface states that in the Locations controlled by the British and godly city of Grahamstown "the death rate has been over fifty per thousand."—A.S.C.

have power to move its readers towards a vivid perception of what there is to be gained for Native life by Segregation—the callousness of the South African Dominion as to her town mortality having been apparently so appalling where Natives have been concerned.

This correspondent of *The Friend*, it may be remarked, writes in no unprecedented fashion. So might some dusky exponent of Anti-Semitic statecraft have written in the Egypt of Moses' time. The outlook expressed is worthy of a Lacedæmonian expounding the traditionally relentless policy[1] of Sparta's oligarchy towards the aboriginal Helot population of Laconia. Dr. Schalkwyck does not indeed propound to us the secret murder-gang expedient of the Krypteia, by which a few marked men of the Helots were put out of the way from time to time. Why should he? He pins his faith to liquor and syphilis: he is very confident that such periodical massacres of innocents as our slum conditions are so apt at contriving will continue to occur.

> " Live thou, whose infamy is not thy fame!
> Live, fear no heavier chastisement from me!
> . . . . . .
> But be thyself and know thyself to be!
> And ever at thy season be thou free
> To spill the venom when thy fangs o'erflow."

It has been said truly enough that the blood of the martyrs is to be accounted the seed of the Church, may not the venom-spilth of this doctrinaire repres-

[1] " Sparta always feared her Helots, and it was essential to keep an enemy out of Laconia."—W. E. Heitland, " Agricola."

sionist and his tribe be the fruitful seed of a movement in Anglo-Africa—a movement on its negative side of honest impatience with our present Policy of Exploitation, and on its positive side of genuine reaction towards a Policy affording to Native African life ample and acceptable land-areas on which to exercise its freedom of self-development? These words from the Union of South Africa have a prophetic menace as to our Native Land Areas Question in His Majesty's Colony of Southern Rhodesia: "We want to be loyal, but as things are moving we have less and less land in which to be loyal."

It is now about forty years since Leo Tolstoy chose that title, "What then must we do?" for one of his books—a title that in its interrogation awoke ringing echoes of the New Testament. Is not the call of the New Testament religion, the religion of Jesus, to bear one another's burdens, and not to be ourselves burdens to others, expressed with disconcerting candour in that Russian publicist's comment on anti-social life? "I sit on a man's neck, weighing him down and making him carry me, and yet assure myself and others that I pity him, and greatly wish to ease his lot by all possible means—except by getting off his back."

"What I believe in is a greater and larger-heartedness in the people of this country," General Smuts, then the Prime Minister of United South Africa's Dominion, told us quite recently. "We are too much in the grasp of preconceived notions about the superiority, the claims of the white man, and so on." Quite so! It is by this time abundantly clear that the claims of our dominant Anglo-Dutch race to play Old-Man-of-the-Sea to the Native Races' Sindbad have been stretched inconsiderately and quite unduly.

"I say deliberately," said Lord Selborne, when he was speaking of one great branch of the South African Native family, "that the King has no more loyal subjects . . . and that the one thing they most desire is to be left alone."

"What Then Must We Do?" The late Bishop Frank Weston, of Zanzibar, a Philo-African who was also a statesman, told us out of the fullness of his experience in the Eastern part of Central Africa what we must *not* do if we would remain loyal to the idea of a British Commonwealth. In an article in the *Empire Review* of October, 1924, published about a month before his own death in Africa, he wrote: "It is no good service to the Empire to sacrifice the health and social life of the Africans[1] to a few thousand Englishmen who find land-owning cheaper in Africa than in England and less exhausting than in Canada or Australia. Settlers are needed in Africa; but in small numbers, and of picked character. To open Africa to all comers irrespective of the needs of the rest of the Empire is to shorten the Empire's existence."

Freedom to live your own life in your own rural areas with your own Race's ideals in sight—that is

[1] Cf. what Edwin W. Smith says in "The Golden Stool": "The Belgians asked themselves: 'Are we not on the way to kill, slowly or quickly, according to circumstances, but surely, the goose that lays the golden eggs?'"—A.S.C.

not so very much of a boon to ask after all. And the grant of that boon may mean, may it not, just the difference between a race's future daybreak, and a race's present darkness ?

What then must we do ?

What indeed, but use patience in bearing one another's burdens, and in practising and preaching a forbearance that will refuse to super-impose the exceeding heavy burden of our own Race's egotism on subject Races ! There has been much talk about Segregation in the sub-continent of South Africa, but are we prepared to be equitable in any scheme of South African Segregation, whether in the Union of South Africa (where it is comparatively hard[1] to be in any real sense equitable as to a Division of the Land) or in South Rhodesia (where it may be found comparatively easy) ?

Have we not, we few members of Anglo-Africa's white oligarchy, powers reposed in us by Providence, powers over foul and fair weather in public affairs more formidable than any of those[2] imputed to the rain-makers and storm-dispersers of the races which we rule ?

[1] Cf. a letter by the Rev. F. B. Rand, S.S.M., in *The Rand Daily Mail* of January 18th, 1923—the writer says : " That is the whole point of our contention, viz., that the white man has seized (and is still seizing the little that remains !) practically the whole of the land, and has so rendered the territorial separation of the races an impossibility—unless, indeed, he is prepared at this late hour to disgorge and make restitution. . . . The existing Native reserves, we are told, are only too small because of the ' feckless and improvident agriculture.' Let your correspondent take up a map and see the utter disproportion of the land allotted to white and black. Not one fiftieth of it is in the hands of the Native, and yet they outnumber the Europeans by five to one ! "

[2] Cf. " The Magical Control of the Weather," in Sir James Frazer's " The Golden Bough " (abbreviated edition).

Assuredly our interference or our apathy may be much to blame, if the skies of our Anglo-African States are destined to become red and lowering before long now with every portent of foul weather to follow. On the other hand, success may largely be due to the exercise of hope and good-will by members of a dominant Race, should any Segregation Policy succeed in bringing daybreak to a racially benighted sub-continent.

In that " Pandora's Box " drama, which now holds the South African stage, we want some really spirited Policy to play the part of Hope, if tragic issues are to be mercifully averted. The reader may remember the story of Pandora coming down to earth, and being taken by Epimetheus in wedlock for better for worse, for richer for poorer. This is how Kingsley tells that story : " There came . . . the most beautiful creature that ever was seen, Pandora by name, which means All the gifts of the Gods. But she had a strange box in her hand. . . . And they opened the box between them, of course, to see what was inside. . . .And out flew all the ills which flesh is heir to. . . . But one thing remained at the bottom of the box and that was Hope." Is not our old-fashioned British Idealism an odd match for Anglo-Dutch Africa (with her beauty and her mysteriously sinister past), as odd as Epimetheus was for Pandora when they kept house together in the time-honoured tale ? Had not Pandora's Box of Mystery a certain kinship with South Africa's Native-and-Immigrant Problem ? Is there any practicable Policy but a Segregation Policy that can rise to the present great occasion and play Hope's heroic rôle? Dr. S. M. Molema, the Bantu historian of his own Race, has praised cautiously, and in no reckless spirit, an equitable scheme of Segregation: "Such a scheme, if equitably carried out, would be highly satisfactory, and in that way can the dangers of 'the Native problem' that exists for the whites and 'the foreign problem' that exists for the blacks be considerably minimized and perhaps successfully combated." But let us not forget that an enlightened Segregation Policy implies Faith, not the egotistical Faith that insists on superimposing one's own Race's Kultur on a subject Race, but Faith in Freedom and so in the grant of Freedom for its self-development to that subject Race. Creative Imperialism (of the Higher or Christian type) is surely at its supreme height of power when, refraining from the temptation to mould temptingly plastic subjects, it affords them a scope and a sphere wherein to mould themselves.

PART II

NOTES ON NATIVE AREAS IN SOUTHERN RHODESIA AND ON THAT FREEDOM OF SELF-DEVELOPMENT WHICH OUGHT TO BE ALLOWED TO THEM

INDEX

[" But when the native in his leopard skin or his brilliant cotton blanket, when his woman with her load on her head and her child slung across her back, stride erect and with free, swinging movement along a red and unwrought road ; and the sun makes sharp yellows and blacks ; and the sky is a fierce blue above them—not a serene blue, but a burning, angry blue ; and the barren, rusty mountains, crested with rock, and crudely curved and angled as if God Himself had turned modernist, form their background ; *then* the Kaffir and his Africa are one, and there is that before the eyes to make a painter immortal."—Mrs. S. G. Millin, " The South Africans."]

CHAPTER VIII

AN AFRICA OF THE AFRICANS

CHAPTER VIII

["Can you not see with others' eyes as yet ?
Will not your home-love take their home-love's hand?
You that have lusted for your own green land
In exile, you that in her war-time set
Life on her altar, you that waive regret
For fallen friends—fallen so she might stand,
You that, far-banished, fond returns have planned,
You that her smiles remember, frowns forget !
O look in your own heart, and should you find
England's own name indelible and clear—
By England's love I charge you, be more kind
To such wild tribes as hold their few hills dear !
Filching your half of their wild hills away,
Leave them their half to live their fathers' way."]

WE pass on to consider the Native Areas that such a Segregation Policy as we have advocated proposes to create. Our point of view is that every Native Area in colonized Africa should be safeguarded as an inviolable sanctuary which may shelter African tribal life, and foster its self-development. In the Natal Segregation treatise we have quoted, the writer speaks of insight gained by the Natal Native Commission, whereon he himself served, into the Native's apparent point of view. He says, "The underlying note of much of the Native evidence was too much contact with Europeans, and too much interference with their life by Government and its agents, especially the police.[1] Indeed if we could get at the hearts of the people, consciously, sub-consciously or unconsciously, we would find the desire to be let alone. Why is the white man constantly disturbing us ? "

The Colonist writer in his recommendations sets himself to remove this, as well as other alleged grievances, by the policy of Segregation that he advocates. He says : " It will be patent to those who have followed me thus far that the underlying principles of the recommendation I am now making is the separation of the races to an extent hitherto never attempted, the preservation of the home life, and race integrity, and the prevention of race overlapping, contact and conflict. They will therefore be prepared to admit that there should be no violation by the white man of the areas set apart for the Abantu. Only those would be admitted as residents into these reserves who were there primarily for the benefit of the Natives, administrative officers, missionaries and teachers. Trading licenses issued during pleasure and speci-

[1] The Natal Rebellion was dated 1906. Mr. Evans has recorded that " Since Natal took over responsible Government in 1893 no less than forty-eight new laws specially applicable to the Native population were passed and many new regulations framed under these and previous laws. These laws and regulations pressed upon the daily life of the Native on all sides. . . ." Responsibly governed S. Rhodesia would do well to be warned by what happened in responsibly governed Natal. Already has been heard a Native's criticism that the change from Chartered Co. Government in S. Rhodesia was a change for the worse apparently, as meaning more laws. In 1925 a S. Rhodesian Native Education Commission actually recommended that it should be made penal to harbour a goat or a calf in a Native's sleeping-hut. Will it next be proposed to penalize the distribution of Christmas cards representing Jesus Christ as housed in a cattle-byre throughout Mashonaland ? Where will such humourless pettiness be likely to stop ? A. S. C.

fically conferring no vested interests might be allowed, but the idea is that the natives shall in time, under guidance, be fitted to fulfil all the duties pertaining to their separate existence. Within the native areas a black man will have many rights and privileges; two obligations will however be absolutely imperative; the broad policy governing his affairs must be dictated by the white man through his parliament, and he must be absolutely loyal to the central government, which is in turn responsible to the empire, and in a wide sense to the civilized world at large.

" So, and contingent thereon, a generous policy may well be adopted, making the black man's land one attractive to him,[1] freeing him there from the irritation and overlordship of individual whites, and giving him every opportunity for personal and race development. But outside this domain and within the area of the white race he has no such privileges. Should he go there for any purpose, he must conform and submit to laws and regulations made by the white man for the benefit of the white man."

Obviously our Natal writer is indicating a policy that may even now belatedly ease, if not exactly remove, any present or potential friction between settlers from Europe, or their descendants, and the Natives of Africa in the States of the South African Union. Moreover, there is a like glimmer of hope in his

[1] Mr. Alfred Drew, ex-Native Commissioner, some time ago drew attention in a Southern Rhodesian paper—*The Independent*—to the question of giving the Native reasonable liberty in the Reserves as to hunting or trapping game. He instanced a case of a duiker being taken in a Native hunting-net—as to which the S. Rhodesian Law Department had ruled that there was a case for prosecution. A. S. C.

suggestions for African territories, lying north of the Union border-line—that are already more or less affected by a similar friction. Colonized or Europeanized Africa hangs together and offers the same type of riddle in more than one latitude.

What I want to argue in detail is the call to secure a vantage-ground for African self-development in the Native Areas of Southern Rhodesia—the only part of Africa that I know comparatively well of my own personal knowledge. My remarks apply primarily to Native Reserves already demarcated, but they are likely to have some bearing on Native Land Purchase Areas which it is proposed to create and to group with them in the near future.

It is vastly important that the blessed institution of Native Areas should be safeguarded if it is to afford a real break-wind and make-shift harbour of refuge for the natural and legitimate instincts of the African's race consciousness. Was it not said of a Celtic race that their speech they would keep, their land they would lose—except wild Wales? Who would deny the value of Wales to the British Empire in particular, and to the world at large, as a preserve of Celtic aspirations?

If one believes, and I take it a good many Europeans are at one with me in believing that Africans have racial characteristics well worth fostering, one is apt to appreciate the potential value of Reserved Areas in such places as South or East or Central Africa, and the importance of safeguarding them. One way to look at Native Reserves is surely as wind-screens tempering the blustering overseas breeze to the shorn black lamb. Assuredly they may serve, too, if only they be rightly safeguarded, as islands or harbours wherein African tribal life may develop largely on its own lines. On the other hand there is a real Post-War danger of Native Reserved Areas being used to subserve a sort of Anglo-Saxon Imperial efficiency programme—a programme that makes for Prussianization of sorts—for the imposition of Kultur, or its equivalent, upon a weaker coloured race by a stronger white race. Ancient Imperial History supplies plain warnings as to the public danger which may attend on a movement with the innocent-sounding title of "Empire Resources Development." A student of Agriculture and Rustic life in the Greco-Roman World has told us a conclusion he has formed. "I believe that the maladies from which the old Greco-Roman civilization suffered, and which in the end brought about its decay and fall, were directly or indirectly due to this taint more than to any other cause. I know of no case ancient or modern in which a people have attained to a sound and lasting prosperity by exploiting the servitude of other men. Serfdom or slavery, it matters not" (W. E. Heitland, "Agricola"). The writer of a well-known novel represented his hero as giving "efficiency" a bad name, meaning, so it seemed to him, being unkind to someone weaker than yourself, and getting the law on your side while you are engaged in the job. Yes, getting the law on your side, and pleading "efficiency" is an attitude that seriously threatens African self-development. Those who care for Africans need to be vigilant in these Post-War times, as recognizing what an attractive country Africa must appear to the reactionaries of Europe in certain important aspects. Are not her labour and her land, so massive in quantity, so easy of manipulation, alluring to capitalists of a certain type, who find both land and labour[1] to be scarce and unmanageable nearer home ?

In February, 1925, a Southern Rhodesian paper reported an interview with a big business ambassador, who expressed himself sanguinely as to that Conservative Government which was ruling Home and Colonies for Imperial Britain. He said : " You have a Government which is peculiarly sympathetic towards the development of overseas resources." That sounds fair enough, does it not ? We need not be disturbed by such an announcement. Yet some later reported remarks of the same envoy have not quite the same innocent sound : " It is no secret that South Africa seems to be attracting more interest to-day than any other part of the world. The public are realizing that it is virtually the last undeveloped reserve for raw material supplies, and, comparatively speaking, the last untapped source of native labour supplies." Such a one-sided capitalistic way of looking at her, as is exemplified by this last sentence, has been the curse of Africa too long already.

I want to emphasize three points in this chapter

[1] A Rhodesian advertising brochure recently issued in connection with the Empire Exhibition states : " One advantage which all reap is a plentiful supply of inexpensive labour." It goes on to reassure its readers as to Rhodesia so far having " no eight hours' day."

that require vigilant attention : (1) Arts and Crafts ; (2) Public Works ; (3) Pass Laws. Two other points—Encroachments on Native Areas and Rates without Representation may best be dealt with in other chapters.

(1) We were confronted some while ago in Southern Rhodesia with a somewhat elaborate scheme for developing Native industries on our Native Reserves. A Director of Native Development was appointed, and Arts and Crafts for Natives were subjects he proposed to handle. As it turned out, his energy was diverted, and for the time he found outlets for that energy in other directions.[1] Before his appointment he had been Native Commissioner in a comparatively backward or primitive District, and he was able to expound clearly his ideas of the Native's need and capability of progress. A great danger of his scheme in regard to various matters seemed to me to lurk in the temptation that might assail him or his successors to rely on the prestige of our European Government and to superimpose the dogmatism of Europe on Reserves that should serve as strongholds of African self-development. For Native Arts and Crafts should evolve their own developments : European supervision and invigilation may easily be carried to excess, and may conceivably worsen them rather than better them from an artist's point of view. Dr. S. M. Molema in his book, " The Bantu—Past and Present," says : " That skill which the Bechuana

[1] In the development of Government Central Schools of a useful type for Mashonaland and Matabeleland. A. S. C.

section of the Bantu displayed in carving and decorating wood to all shapes and forms by means of the crudest instruments is gone, and now, provided with easily manipulated knives and chisels, they could not reproduce their original workmanship. The very poetical compositions which were turned out by the hundred, in every clan, are now a difficult feat in spite of the increased range of Bantu ideas and vocabulary. So is it—through the limited range of Bantu creations, trades and industries. . . . It seems it should be the business of the more advanced to study, uphold, and propagate their national customs and institutions, only modifying or abolishing such as are pernicious, and seem calculated to clash with the best in civilization, and to arrest progress; smoothing those that are jagged, recasting and refining such as are rough and uncouth. It should be their concern to learn first to look upon life through their own national spectacles, and then, but not till then, through foreign spectacles to inculcate into their less advanced brethren the respect and esteem of Bantu usages, while emphasizing only the laudable practices in the new civilization."

Nevertheless much might legitimately be done for Native craftsmen by providing and organizing regular centres for the sale of pottery and basket-work to help the more remote neighbourhoods. Also much might be done (by way of shows, industrial training-courses and demonstrations) to help the husbandmen and graziers of the Native Areas to adjust themselves to altered times. A year or two ago we had a very considerable number of ploughs owned by Natives in our District (2,100 was the estimate) and some wheeled transport: in such a District there is to be found a legitimate scope for an industrial reformer—that of helping traditional iron-craft and wood-crafts to meet the new demands for repairs and replacements of parts, which the dawn of a new era has created.

(2) We in Southern Rhodesia are faced with the imposition of a special burden on the inhabitants of our Native Reserves. I mean the opening-out of those Reserves by roads, and up-keep of those roads when made. I believe that both the Reserves Commission and our late Administrator have advocated, more or less directly, the saddling of our Reserves-dwellers with their roads' maintenance. I would point out that in our late Administrator (Sir Drummond Chaplin)'s own letter bound up with the Reserves Commission's recommendations he excuses the comparatively meagre amounts of educational and medical grants made specifically for Native needs, at a time when Native tax-payers were paying such a large proportion of the Territory's revenue. His plea is that it should be remembered that the Native has a share in the general good government of the Territory. That point being granted, then by all means *let the Native have his proper share of our Public Works Department's assistance on his Native Reserves*. The late Maurice Evans of the Natal Native Commission (which made its researches after the Natal Native Rebellion of 1906) chronicles as one of the "complaints of the ordinary kraal native," "compulsory labour on roads and public works." The inhabitant

of a Native Reserve certainly ought not to be mulcted in corvée labour *without pay and without rations*[1] for the provision of such comparatively elaborate motor roads on his own Reserves as may afford easy access to European visitors. In giving evidence before the S. Rhodesian Lands Commission in September, 1925, the writer suggested that it should be matter of earnest recommendation that if our land is to be divided, the Natives get an approximately fair share of services of Public Works Department, Veterinary Department, and so on. What sort of a share have Natives of Reserves (in that part of Mashonaland I have known for so many years) as yet received ?

(3) I am encouraged to believe that some sort of reaction against the spirit of the South African Pass Laws has lately been in evidence. Modified as the Southern Rhodesian Pass Law has been, its sinister operation as a manufacturer of offences and multiplier of punishments has been denounced again and again by those whose voices should command respect. It seems extraordinary that no more vigorous measures have been taken so far to abate the morbid conditions created by this loathsome law. In May, 1920, General Smuts said at a time when he combined the

[1] Cf. Dr. Norman Leys on Communal Labour in Kenya : " It is just as if the unskilled labour on roads and bridges in rural England had to be done for nothing by the rural workers, each of them liable to be called out for a week in every quarter at the pleasure of the County Council, while all navvying in the towns was paid for at market rates out of taxation borne chiefly by the rural workers."—(Preface to 3rd edition of " Kenya.") Notices in the Native dialects precisely defining the limitations of service, and stating the terms of remuneration, ought to be obtainable from S. Rhodesian Native Commissioners, when Government requisitions labour in the Native Areas of S. Rhodesia. I owe this suggestion to Archdeacon Owen of Kenya.—A.S.C.

offices of Prime Minister in the South African Union and Minister of its Native Affairs : " the Pass laws do the whites no good and are intolerable to the Natives."

The whole subject, raising as it does the question, " Are technical civil offences to be punished as crimes ? " seems to need an essay in itself. Surely the British Imperial Parliament has been familiarized by this time with denunciations of making breach-of-contract offences criminal instead of civil offences in Kenya—where a Pass Law is a comparatively novel institution. When will the Colonial Office speak out about parts of Africa far south of Kenya where the sum of human misery has been lavishly increased for years past by allowing a vicious confusion of criminal and civil matters to establish itself and to prosper in its villainy ? How long is any British Colonial Government to go on tapping freely the fruitful source of revenue that a Native Pass Ordinance provides, both by the lavish ingathering of fines, and by the lavish employment of largely augmented supplies of convict labour ? Does not Imperial Reconstruction demand the sacrifice of such State profiteering as well as other sacrifices ? Earl Buxton said in a Presidential Address to the African Society : " Everyone agrees that the Pass Laws should be reformed and simplified. These laws, although in theory a protection to the raw Kaffir, are undoubtedly a source of provocation and annoyance to the Natives as a whole." Anyhow it would seem to be a modest and workable proposal to obtain one particular measure of Pass

Law Reform at once. I mean the mitigation of Pass Law Regulations so far as they affect Natives on their own Reserves (or within the boundaries of any Territorial Segregation Areas that it is now proposed to create), as distinct from Natives in European Areas. *No* Native ought to be put under arrest, or detained, or punished, for *not* having his Registration Certificate (that flimsy piece of parchment for the replacement of which the Chartered Company Native Department under the old regime has often charged half a sovereign so dishonourably)[1] on his person, or at hand for inspection, night and day, *when he is on his own heath.* I mean when he is on Native ground in a Native African Area.

What the Native has had to suffer in the past when he has left a Southern Rhodesian Native Reserve and sought work in a Southern Rhodesian Urban Area may be gathered from an extract inserted in one of Mr. Alfred Drew's pamphlets pleading for Native Reform[2]:

"The Report of the Cost of Living Committee, after dealing with the cost of living as far as the natives are concerned, proceeds as follows :

A Serious Hardship.

"One other aspect of the Native question brought to the notice of the Committee which, although not

[1] Cf. Clough : "Thou shalt not steal : an empty feat,
When it's so lucrative to cheat."

[2] Mr. Afred Drew acted as Native Commissioner in Victoria and Mazoe Districts. The reference is to a Cost of Living Committee for Southern Rhodesia which has deliberated in quite recent times.

of primary importance from the cost-of-living point of view, deserves to be mentioned is referred to as follows by a witness :

" ' A serious hardship is the fact that, owing to the numerous pass and trespass laws in force in this country, the Native who comes to our towns finds it impossible to avoid the many pitfalls made for him, and becomes an offender over and over again, and having to pay a fine every time he is brought to court, the cost of his living is increased in a way that, to say the least, is undesirable. As it is generally considered necessary to have these statutory prohibitions and regulations, it seems to me that magistrates should recognize the hardships involved in paying large—that is, relatively large—fines upon conviction of these offences which really involve no turpitude, and if the magistrates of the country were circularized to this effect, this undue increase in the cost of the Natives' living might be lessened. Personally, I think the fine should be very small for this kind of offence: half a crown or five shillings seems to me quite enough. In this way, also Natives are given a chance of avoiding gaol and the number of recidivists is kept down.'

" I think this is a serious matter. By following a policy of pin-pricks we make the working Native's life a burden and increase the growing ill-will towards the Empire, a feeling which is spreading every day. I dare say 90 per cent. of the native ' boys '[1] who

[1] This was in the old Chartered Company days. But honour to whom honour is due ! The Chartered Company at any rate was not responsible for that Native Juveniles Measure, which passed its third read-

come to our towns to work have seen the inside of the gaol as the result of breaking one of the many onerous pass and trespass laws, for which the fines imposed have been too heavy."

In conclusion it may be well to recapitulate the ideals that animate the Native Areas policy we have been advocating in this chapter. We want a racially self-conscious African not to feel himself homeless in a colonized Africa; we want a miniature Africa of the Africans, free, as far as may be, from exploitation, and free, as far as may be, for self-development, to exist

ing in the S. Rhodesian Legislative Assembly recently. "This measure which Mr. Amery is to be asked to sanction carries with it all those repugnant elements which attach to malodorous systems of indentured labour of adults. These juveniles are to be liable to fines, the boy children to whipping—and whipping, be it noted, without prior reference either to a magistrate on the grounds of justice or to a doctor as to the physical fitness of the child labourer to bear the flogging. It is doubtful whether such drastic powers have ever been conferred upon officials before to indenture pauper or orphan children. The official under this Act may dispose of the juvenile practically as he likes, for there is no stipulation as to the child's willingness to accept or refuse a six months' indenture; indeed, Clause 10 of the Act provides flogging for refusal."—Letter of Mr. John H. Harris, printed in *The Manchester Guardian* of January 20th, 1927. "The seriousness of the Act is clearly demonstrated by the fact that the League of Nations has just laid it down that forced labour for private gain is slavery."—Mr. Alfred Holt in *No More War*, April, 1927. The Rhodesian Agricultural Union Conference's Resolution No. 4 in 1925 ran as follows: "That native piccanins be indentured or in some way be brought under the provision of the Masters and Servants Act." The powers given to contract Native female juveniles by this Measure are arguably appalling. But for its skilful gilding of philanthropy it is scarcely conceivable that the Colonial Office would have swallowed it in its entirety. Mr. Hadfield, M.L.A., pointed out to the S. Rhodesian Legislative Assembly when it was under discussion "that the Bill was originally intended to protect the Native juvenile, but it now seemed to be regarded as offering facilities for wholesale juvenile labour."—(*Rhodesia Herald*, November 5th, 1926.) On April 4th, 1927, the Prime Minister of S. Rhodesia told an R.A.U. Congress: "One thing arose out of the Congress of 1925. We have now got, not without difficulty, on the Statute-book the Native Juvenile Apprenticeship Act." The text of the Act itself may repay the study of English readers, and explain some of that difficulty to which Sir C. Coghlan referred. A.S.C.

within the borders of every one of our Native Areas. From the point of view of the Higher (or Christian) Imperialism African Native Areas ought to be properly safeguarded,[1] so that on them Africans may be free to go about their proper business of preparing Africa's own distinctive contribution to the city of God, and of bringing Africa's own unique "glory and honour into it."

[1] Under the new Native Department Bill (1927) as drafted, it is actually proposed to remove an existing safeguard. Clause 17 "is a departure from the law as it stood while the British South Africa Company were governing Rhodesia. That law provided that an alleged offence against a Native Commissioner should not be tried by himself but by somebody else."

CHAPTER IX

A PLEA AGAINST ENCROACHMENTS

CHAPTER IX

" Back to the land is the cry in the older countries, where they have experienced the dire results of exaggerated city life, and the thought of the best among them is to replace, by more natural conditions, what has insidiously developed into a cancer in their national life. Here we have a people crying aloud against the divorce threatening them. Along the line of the genius of a race much may be done, much may be modified, wounds may be healed, and development and progress made possible; counter to it, dire distress and eventual destruction of the race ideal. Of infinite import and value to the Abantu race has been this clinging to the land and all that it implied. It has preserved them from the dissolution which a too ready compliance with the temptations held out by our civilization would have implied. The race still stands firm; its attachment to the land has saved it."—MAURICE EVANS' " Black and White in South-East Africa."

" There are who lord it o'er their fellow-men
With most prevailing tinsel: who unpen
Their baaing vanities to browse away
The comfortable green and juicy hay
From human pastures. . . ."—JOHN KEATS.

QUITE a number of us now are in favour of some or other form of segregation policy, securing to Africans such right of self-development, in accordance with the genius of their own race, as a race ought to possess. Quite a number of us do not want this race of husbandmen and herdsmen to be divorced from that soil on which they lavish such a real, if in part uninstructed, affection from generation to generation.

Any arbitrary and unwarranted interference on the part of our Government, or of ourselves as individuals, which may result in the divorce of the two parties who have contracted a union of long standing may quite reasonably be regarded as an outrage against the welfare of our community as a whole. But if we refuse to countenance any such divorce, are we right in giving our approval to an outrage of a different kind, a detestable outrage if only it be viewed in its own true light and not masked or camouflaged ?

In one of the Jacobean dramas, recently revived on the English stage—Beaumont's and Fletcher's "The Maid's Tragedy"—the main interest hinges on a situation created in defiance of good faith, of honour, and of equity. Evadne, one of the principal characters in the play, is represented as being the secret mistress of a reigning monarch. She is made over to a loyal subject of his in lawful wedlock, with the secret understanding, unknown to her duped husband, that she is to hold herself at her royal paramour's disposal, more or less as of old. The subsequent action of the drama moves relentlessly towards such a catastrophe as this repulsive desecration of the marriage tie has invited.

While deploring the calamitous curtailment of Native Reserve land by our Reserves Delimitation Order in Council of November, 1920, and regretting the failure of those in authority so far to carry out, fairly and adequately, our Chief Native Commissioner's Native Land-Purchase Areas' proposals, submitted to our Legislative Council some years ago, I should be inclined to question whether Southern Rhodesian natives are not really more menaced at present by movements to make their marriage to their native communal lands a mock marriage than by any movements to divorce them from their own native soil. The position of residents on the Southern Rhodesian Native Reserves threatens to resemble the position of that wronged husband in the Jacobean tragedy—a position in which one's own in name is not one's own in fact, inasmuch as it is left at some over-ruling power's disposal, a power that is much too prone to be used arbitrarily and unwarrantably at reasonable liberty's expense.

In an article entitled, "An Africa of the Africans" ("International Review of Missions," January, 1921), I wrote as to our newly created Director of Native Development's activities:

"This new Government scheme of ours has already involved the choice of about 700 acres from one reserve to serve the purpose of an industrial school farm. Now this is to create a dangerous precedent. . . . Such areas should be chosen near to native reserves, but not on them."

It would now appear that my apprehension as to the creation of a dangerous precedent was justified to some extent. In an Annual Report of that Missionary Society (the Society for the Propagation of the Gospel) which has supported my own work in Africa, I have found the following information recorded:

"There is, in Southern Rhodesia, a Native Development Department in the care of two Government officials. . . . Part of their work is concerned with two industrial schools started by the Government three years ago, and to which missionaries were specially appointed as principals during the past year. . . . It is hoped that, later on, some of the most successful boys will be granted small model farms on the Reserve adjoining the School, and thus become the pioneers in their own area of a class of settled and progressive farmers." Why *on* the reserve, and not on land *near it, but outside its already diminished acreage*, I would like to have explained to me. There need surely have been no real difficulty in securing an appropriate permanent site for Demboshawa Government School adjacent to Chindamora Native Reserve, instead of on it, nor in finding sites for "small model farms" contiguous to such a site, and so to the Reserve itself. *Has not some land lopped off that Reserve in accordance with the Order in Council of* 1920 *been offered for sale quite recently?* Why should the common land of the people be liable to be subjected to gratuitous encroachments? How much land, one would like to ask, is likely to be left for the genuinely free self-development of the rank and file of our Native population at this rate? Where will raw Natives and ordinary Mission-taught Natives find room if a few promising Government School pupils are to be allowed to absorb even small-sized model-farms in our Native Reserves, which are presumably given to be held in communal (as for the present the most appropriate) tenure by various populous Tribes under the High Commissioner's trusteeship?

I submit that what is really wanted in the way of African industrial progress is such genuine self-development from below, among themselves, and on their own lines, as one has noted from time to time among the Natives of Charter District, Mashonaland, during this present generation. Their agricultural system has been markedly transformed by the rapid adoption of the plough in many parts of the District. One has the expert testimony of Charter District's Native Commissioner (given in the Southern Rhodesian Chief Native Commissioner's Annual Report presented to our Legislative Council in the year 1921) as to the way in which a new order of social conditions has evolved itself in the District which he has directed for so many years already[1]. What he says is this: "A large section of the able-bodied men are energetic agriculturists, and may be styled successful farmers in the district, and as long as there is a demand for their products they will not work for Europeans where long hours, low wages, and routine work[2] prevail."

[1] He was appointed Head of it in the year 1902.

[2] I note that two correspondents of *The Rhodesian Herald* of Dec. 24th, 1926, are not so polite as our N.C.: "At present in most farm compounds the natives live under far less attractive conditions than they do when at home. They have a lesser variety of food, and their surroundings are often more unhealthy and insanitary than polite words can describe." So says one: the other is even more outspoken. He speaks of "the treatment that the native too often receives when he does go out to work: the unconcealed contempt, aversion, and hatred; the epithets, curses and blows. And why? As often as not because the native knows but little English and his master is too frankly contemptuous of all things native to even attempt to learn his tongue. Why? 'Because he's a native and must be kept in his place.' One thing I know: that if I were a native nothing on earth would induce me (willingly) to work for the majority of white employers."

Shame to him who thinks ill and not well of such a phase in present-day African's self-development as that to which these words of Mr. J. W. Posselt, N.C., testify!

Under Government Notice 206, published in a Southern Rhodesian "Government Gazette," under date 18th May, 1923, S. Rhodesia's late Administrator (for the B.S.A. Company) was authorized to set aside with the High Commissioner's approval, such areas within any Native Reserve as he might "consider necessary for the erection of buildings, and providing other facilities for native administration, the police, native hospitals, educational and such other purposes as may be required from time to time in the interests of the natives."

As to Mission sites, a real menace to Native Reserve acreage is contained in the provision that a grant of a site not exceeding 50 morgen[1] may be made to any Mission Society (recognized by the Administration) of a permit of occupation or a lease, on the recommendation of the Chief Native Commissioner. I am glad to understand that the Native Commissioner of Charter District in Mashonaland has made a representation that most of the various Native Reserves in his District ought not to be regarded as being able to afford 50-morgen sites out of their communal acreages. I was glad too to ascertain from the late General Superintendent of Wesleyan Methodist Church Missions in this Colony that so long as he himself might direct the local policy of his Church he had no

[1] A morgen equals approximately 2⅛ acres.

intention whatever of applying for the grant of any new Mission sites to his Society at the expense of the Native people's tribal Reserves. I am thankful that the Mission Body I served has now accepted a lease of five acres, where it had formally a right to twenty acres in the Manyene Reserve in my own District. The use of Native Teachers domiciled as members of those local village communities, which they may have a commission to teach, is surely a Mission system far less open to objection, where Native Reserves are concerned, than any system of granting considerable slices of land for the establishment of imposing Mission Stations on the common land of the people. As to Police Camps, the Natives' Reserve land ought not to be mulcted to furnish an extensive site (and a possibly yet wider sphere of interference) for the convenience of a Government outpost's establishment; e.g., I would humbly submit that the Wedza Police Camp in Marandellas District, Mashonaland,[1] would be far better situated on an acquired site (such as that half-farm on which the Chimanza Wesleyan Mission is located close by), in the neighbourhood of the Wedza Native Reserve, than absorbing, as it does, a share of the Wedza Native Reserve's delimited area. I would submit

[1] A Missionary, living close by this camp, under date of 1st March, 1924, speaks of the Police and the Native Department "having established a double camp in the Wedza Reserve." He tells me that this establishment has meant a good number of acres for the camps proper, land for grazing cattle (one policeman having had over 150 head at one time) over a wide area, gardens for themselves, and native messengers and police. According to his account, the natives have been driven further and further off into the Reserve "to such an extent that there is practically a Native Department and Police farm around the camp."

that the menace offered to Areas of Reserve land, which before long now may become congested (one Native Reserve in my own District is already comparatively congested) by the discretionary Clause which I have quoted (Number 14) of Government Notice 206 is no slight one. One remembers the description of the personnel of the Chief's following in that Macpherson Raid into the MacTavish country:

> " Four and twenty men
> And five and thirty pipers."

Our Native Reserve land, already severely circumscribed under the settlement declared in our Reserves Order in Council of 9th November, 1920, is now threatened under thc Government Notice of 18th May, 1923, by the prospect of a multiplication of alien immigrants holding some official capacity in connection with Church or State, whose business it may be to teach the unfortunate Reserve Native how to develop what Reserve land has been left to him, not according to the adaptive and imitative genius of his own Race, with its rich stores of traditional wisdom as to local conditions, but according to some superimposed foreign fashion. The Natives have been given a *de jure* prescriptive right to their Reserves, why is their *de facto* right to be jeopardized ? Not long ago I discovered in an English newspaper an article on " Newtakes " (or the stealing of land in old English history), wherein it was stated :

" Lord Thring's Act against unlawful enclosures was passed in 1893, and to-day our remaining common lands, which in England alone cover not less than 1,700,000 acres, are very strictly safeguarded. Commonland can be taken as a site for a church, a school, or a museum, but not more than an acre for any one building. . . ." One would like to see some sensibly thrifty regulation of the same kind made as to discretionary grants with regard to those common lands which have been assigned to be the property of our Native proletariat in Mashonaland and Matabeleland. A really enlightened view of our Public Trusteeship in S. Rhodesia would seem to demand the passing of some such one-acre resolution as that which applies in the Old Country, yes, and *without much delay*, lest a great Public Trust be miserably whittled away. If public opinion of the better sort among South African oligarchs has at last come to recognize the utter inexpediency of pushing the divorce of the son of the soil from the soil to any greater lengths than it has advanced up to the present, can we say that the same public opinion is in no danger of failing to respect our Natives' right to freedom of self-development in their own Areas—Reserve Areas which have been ostensibly dedicated to their own use and enjoyment? Ought not what is theirs in name to be regarded as in a less equivocal sense than it is now, their own in fact?

CHAPTER X

RATING WITHOUT REPRESENTATION

CHAPTER X

[" If ever one were tempted to accept Mr. Balfour's description of the life-history of the human race as 'a brief and discreditable episode in the life of one of the meaner planets' it would be when one reads of the dealings of the white races with the coloured races."—PROFESSOR MURRAY—" Orbis Terrestris."]

AN ex-High Commissioner of South Africa, Earl Buxton, has defined the object and scope of Representative Native Councils such as have been provided for by the Union of South Africa's Native Affairs Act, which came into operation in the year 1920.

In his Presidential Address delivered to the African Society some few months after that Act's inception, he is recorded to have said :

" The object of these Local Councils is to give to the Tribal Natives a real opportunity of managing and being responsible for their own affairs, and of dealing with local matters which affect them, and of enabling them to spend the money they contribute to their own advantage.

" The Local Councils may provide for the construction and maintenance of roads, dams, and drains; the prevention of erosion; for improved water supply; for the suppression of disease of stock by means of dipping tanks; for sanitation and hygiene; for improvement in the method of agriculture and afforestation; for the establishment of hospitals, and especially for educational facilities."

Now under those Draft Letters Patent, which provided for the proposed inauguration of Responsible Government in the Territory of Southern Rhodesia, the legal provision of similar Councils was arranged for, power being given to the Governor-in-Council, subject to the approval of the High Commissioner, at any time after the coming into operation of the proposed Constitution, "to establish by proclamation in any Native Reserve or Reserves such Council or Councils of indigenous Natives representative of the local Chiefs and other Native representatives as may seem to him expedient, for the discussion from time to time of any matters upon which, as being of direct interest or concern to the Native population generally or to any portion thereof, he may desire or ascertain, or they may desire to submit their views. . . .

"It shall also be lawful for the Governor and Council, subject to the like approval, to make regulations conferring on any such Council such powers of management in connection with local matters affecting the indigenous Natives as can in his opinion be safely and satisfactorily undertaken by them. . . ."

The incorporation of such provisions into the new Constitution[1] of His Majesty's Colony of Southern

[1] The Constitution which came into operation on Oct. 1st, 1923, throughout Mashonaland and Matabeleland expressly provides machinery for the establishment of Native Councils.

Rhodesia would seem to be significant. Obviously the advisability of launching some such system in the near future, under which Southern Rhodesia's Natives may be empowered to advise on local matters, and to rate themselves for local purposes, has been foreshadowed by the Imperial Government's express agreement to approve it under certain conditions.

The question remains as to how soon it may be expedient under favourable circumstances for the Governor-in-Council to move in the direction indicated. One fully recognizes the variety of the stages of racial development at which Natives inhabiting various regions of this same Colony (rural or urban, and with or without religious and educational facilities) may be considered to have arrived at the present stage of the Territory's existence. It may, one supposes, be quite plausibly argued that some Southern Rhodesian Native Reserves have already reached the point of development at which the inauguration of local government in their midst would minister to their content, and to their much better corporate organization. As to other Native Reserves, I have no doubt at all that a quite reasonable case to the contrary may be pleaded. My main object in this brief essay is to attack what seems to me a premature and essentially vicious system of rating without representation that has come to life in at least one Native District's Reserves. I would maintain that if our Reserves be not ripe for representation, they are certainly not ripe for rating. I would submit that if rating is now desirable, representation should now be conceded. I would register my well-considered protest against that superimposition of an unconstitutional rating system upon natives with no really representative organization, which has come about already in at least one Native District of Southern Rhodesia. In that particular District, according to our Territory's own Chief Native Commissioner: "Under the law, native cattle have to be dipped the same as those of Europeans; the natives have to pay for this dipping. Representations have been made by chiefs and headmen asking for three additional tanks to be built at their expense, to save long journeys for cattle, and congestion at the existing tanks."

Our Chief Native Commissioner goes on to state that they have also requested the Native Commissioner to purchase for them, from their funds, a certain number of well-bred bulls for the purpose of improving their herds. Moreover, he says of that District's Natives, writing in February of the year 1923, when a famine had been causing very serious want and hardship: "A feeler has been put out amongst them to see whether this is generally acceptable, and, if so, a collection will probably be made in June next, provided the economic conditions have improved sufficiently to justify it. The amount per head has not yet been considered. This money, when collected, will be expended upon the following objects:

"(*a*) Dipping native cattle.

"(*b*) The erection of Dipping Tanks.

"(*c*) The purchase of bulls.

"(*d*) Payment of wages to European supervisor of tanks and adviser to Natives on the care of the bulls and their progeny.

"(*e*) General development of the Reserve for the benefit of the natives."

The "collection" was in due course taken, and taken as it was in the way described, it merited and received severe criticism. It would seem to be perfectly clear that the procedure followed supplied a glaring instance of rating without representation. The present writer is by no means insensitive to the arguments contained in that appeal which the Chief Native Commissioner made to him what time the matter was under discussion. Mr. (now Sir) Herbert J. Taylor, Chief Native Commissioner, wrote: "I have no doubt that you will agree with me that, in the best interests of the Natives, the foregoing objects are worthy of most careful consideration." Nevertheless and notwithstanding such an appeal's clear right to receive consideration, the fact remained that, admirable as the end sought to be attained might be, the right and proper means by which it might have been furthered were not available, and the means actually used were unjustified, inasmuch as they were the sort of means that no end, however admirable, can suffice to justify.

Quite obviously there is no satisfactory machinery in shape at present anywhere in this Territory for gauging the masses' opinions in the back-blocks of any really large Native Reserve. I submit that there is sound reason to believe that grave injustice may be committed under this system of rate collection for alleged improvements by a Native Commissioner, which was inaugurated in this one District of the Province of Mashonaland only a few years ago now. It was pointed out sufficiently plainly by a Southern Rhodesian Native Affairs Commission of some years back that the Native Commissioner of a District, representing as he did the official prestige of the Government, was *not* the proper person to act as the District's labour agent; I submit that the Native Commissioner of a district is *not* the proper person to act as an improvements rate organizer and collector, *and for precisely the same reason.* Rating without representation will not do. Let us then either go backwards or forwards: press forward to the inauguration of representative Native Councils with prerogatives of rating, or retrace this false step lately taken and renounce rating altogether, as far as may be, in every Southern Rhodesian Native Reserve without exception. Let it be frankly admitted that this recent ill-considered inauguration of rating without representation in one of our Mashonaland Native Districts not only menaces African future self-development, but violates a time-honoured and sacred principle of our own English historic freedom. It seems worth while to draw out at some length here the real grounds for the mistrust and apprehension that the adoption of such a policy has excited amongst us.

Caring profoundly as one does for the great mass of illiterate Natives whom this matter may concern, and who are likely to have very little say in this matter, one wishes to state two obvious objections to that

Native Reserves' rate collection policy which has been inaugurated in the Marandellas District.

(1) "No man can serve two masters."

The proposal to raise comparatively large sums, without legislative enactment, from Natives on our Native Reserves, Natives who are already hard put to it to discharge their legal responsibilities to the Government, raises a big question, on which our Legislative Assembly's elected members and our Imperially-appointed Governor should alike have something to say.

The analogy of rate-collecting from a population that already pays taxes may be urged, I suppose. But *until* Natives on our reserves have the same sort of local self-government powers conferred on them that Transkei Natives possess, I submit that such an argument is utterly misleading. Rating without representation is an evil precedent for any one District to set other Districts in our Territory.

(2) Something may, indeed, be said on behalf of our Native Department's rough-and-ready methods already employed for raising the bare necessities of a Native Reserves co-operative dipping trust, i.e., for obtaining funds just sufficient to enable Reserve Natives[1] to meet the requirements of that Cattle Cleansing Ordinance which has become part of the law of our land. These methods of raising dipping

[1] Natives located on Europeans' land may fare much more expensively as regards dipping obligations. A Native Commissioner of Belingwe, Matabeleland, is reported in *The Bulawayo Chronicle* of 17th November, 1923, as follows: "Mr. Bullock instanced the case of a native paying a penny per head per week for dipping. That was 4s. 4d. a year. The native beast was worth nominally 15s., so that

funds, which have already established themselves on our Native Reserves, have at least this much to be urged in their defence, that they have been devised to meet the legal requirements of a properly sanctioned Ordinance. *But* the debatable luxuries of expensive European supervision, of Stock improvement experiments and of other unspecified expenditures alleged to be beneficial, certainly ought *not* to be made to fall on the Native Reserves in any one district at the mere *ipse dixit* of some doubtless well-meaning Native Commissioner, who has managed to obtain the Chief Native Commissioner's sanction or conditional sanction. Native Commissioners are liable, like the rest of us, to be affected by that "last infirmity of noble mind"! They are assuredly no more immune than the rest of us from the common temptation to superimpose reforms by authority, reforms that might be much better attained by the patient fostering of self-development.

I would conclude with a humble request for the study of English history which bears on this vexed question of raising funds by official suasion rather than by legislative enactment. The stories of Tudor "benevolences" and Stuart "ship-money," two useful institutions for raising money without facing the music of elected members in a Parliament, seem to me to be strictly relevant in this connection.

the native was paying insurance at the rate of 30 per cent. per annum. He did not think any insurance company would have the audacity to ask such a rate. 'Some of these natives are walking about without so much as a decent sporran; they cannot even buy a strip of limbo,' said the speaker."

Our Chief Native Commissioner assured me in a letter, dated 21st February, 1923: "There is no question of making a forced levy." Let it be granted then that a Native Commissioner, acting in his capacity as a super-paramount chief, is only entitled to invite appropriate contributions. But will natives inhabiting a Native Reserve find it so very much easier to refuse assessments to a Native Commissioner than merchants or tradesmen in Old England found it to refuse a benevolence to King Henry the Seventh?

I may be excused if I own to having my doubts as to the facilities afforded them for refusal.[1]

In Earl Buxton's account of that system of Native Councils which the Union Native Affairs Act gives power to inaugurate, the importance of one provision calculated to popularize the system amongst primitive taxpayers is duly stressed: "One very important provision of the Act is finance. At present, the ordinary native, living under tribal conditions, pays £2 a year per head as hut tax. Under the provisions of the Act, the Local Council can expend on the

[1] An old-established Rhodesian offers in *The Rhodesian Herald* of 11th January, 1924, a rather significant suggestion for Rating without Representation. He says: "The native mind cannot understand this policy; what he does understand is that what the 'Inkose' thinks right he does! I understand a levy of 9d. per head pays the dipping for a year. Why not make the levy 1s. 3d. and buy bulls with the balance?" Charmingly simple, is it not, this system of raising money without a Parliamentary sanction? Mr. R. M. Archdale, writing in *The Rhodesian Herald* of Christmas Eve, 1926, says: "An old native from the Magondi reserve once said to me, 'The Matabele, when they came, killed us outright when they could, but they didn't kill us all. You white men, you tax us and our wives, you tax our dogs, and you tax our cattle, and none escape. We preferred the Matabele.'" The fact that Natives in S. Rhodesia have had to face not only the devil of taxation, but also the deep sea of arbitrary rating may help to explain such a preference. A. S. C.

above purposes an amount up to £1 per head a year. To the extent that they spend money on these local matters up to twenty shillings[1] the Government taxation will be reduced. The expenditure of the Local Councils on these purposes will therefore not be additional to, but in substitution of, existing taxation." This arrangement obviously compares very favourably with the arrangement we have described under which the Marandellas Natives have been both taxed and also assessed.

"The old order changeth, yielding place to new," "That which decayeth and waxeth old is ready to vanish away." Rating without Representation in the Native Districts of Mashonaland is one of those practices which is ripe for replacement. It is high time that such a system as has persisted in a District I could name if I wished to—a District of Mashonaland more remote than Marandellas—*the system of feudal-bluff, as I may term it, by which a big Native Development Fund has been secured by the Native Commissioner's arbitrary commandeering of the hides of cattle killed by Natives for that arguably "benevolent" purpose, should come to an end.* It is a wonder that such a system

[1] Mr. N. H. Wilson has suggested in the "S. Rhodesian Native Affairs Department Annual" (December, 1923) the entrusting of our proposed S. Rhodesian Native Councils with "the levying of a rate not to exceed 25 per cent. of the native tax, and spending of funds so raised." If the poll tax on males here be £1 per head, with a 10s. additional tax on wives added to a first wife, in comparison with the Union rebate, which has been provided for by the Union Native Affairs Act, this suggestion does not appear to be a very dazzlingly generous one. But did Mr. Wilson mean that there should be any Tax rebate at all? I cherish the hope that one who knows the press of taxation on Natives as he does is in favour of a rebate now, whatever his views were when he wrote his "N.A.D.A." article.

should have shown such hardihood in survival. It is to be hoped that the new Government of Southern Rhodesia, which has made such a good beginning in Native Policy by consecrating Native Reserve revenues to Native Reserve improvement purposes, may see its way to follow the example set by the Union of South Africa's Government, and to decrease the local taxation (in Southern Rhodesia's case a £1 poll tax for males [not specially exempted]—*males whose earning capacity may in many cases be as low as* 5s.[1] *with food per month, and* 10s. *for each extra wife of the taxpayer if he has more wives than one*) in exact proportion to the increase of rating for Reserve improvements adopted by our Natives' own representative Councils of a now not far-distant future. Meanwhile the abuses I have exposed in this chapter need removal. Little though my book may accomplish in other respects, I hope it may do something to expedite matters with regard to their investigation and disappearance. Surely Publicity will providentially avail to remove certain of those abuses in Africa, which the comfortable notions held by colonial administrators that nobody knows, or nobody cares, tend to perpetuate.

[1] Piccanins of 14 are liable to be reckoned as adult males: the 5s. would be exclusive of rations as a rule.

CHAPTER XI

NATIVE AGRICULTURE IN S. RHODESIA

CHAPTER XI

> " Ill fares the land, to hast'ning ills a prey,
> Where wealth accumulates, and men decay ;
> Princes and lords may flourish, or may fade ;
> A breath can make them, as a breath has made ;
> But a bold peasantry, their country's pride,
> When once destroy'd, can never be supplied."
>
> GOLDSMITH

ARE our Natives in Mashonaland unlikely to take advantage of ample and acceptable Areas? Have we a peculiarly inefficient Peasantry to deal with ? I do not believe either of these suggestions for a moment. Possibly that Charter District of Mashonaland in which I have lived is a part of the Territory particularly noticeable for agricultural enterprise. In our Chief Native Commissioner's Annual Report presented in 1925, this District easily leads all other Districts in Southern Rhodesia as to estimated acreage under cultivation with its 103,000 acres, and as to probable yield of bags of grain with its 246,000 bags. Moreover, it has an estimated number of 67,532 cattle, and an estimated number of 2,100 ploughs. As to Charter District's land-hunger, reference may be made to the emphatic Native evidence tendered to our Lands Commission when it visited this District in May, 1925. The fact that there was a rumour abroad in the District that Prince Edward of Wales would make some statement about our Land Question on the occasion of his expected visit to The Range, Charter District, in July, 1925, may surely be regarded as a significant fact. The testimony of Charter's Native Commissioner to a large section of the able-bodied men being energetic agriculturists has been already quoted. As to what he said about employment as labourers for Europeans proving unattractive where long hours, low wages, and routine work prevailed, I would hazard a guess that farm work for Europeans has often been made particularly unattractive in this particular District, which has for its capital the Dutch centre of Enkeldoorn. It is well for us to remember a terse remark of Booker Washington's in this connection: "There is all the difference in the world between working and being worked."

But I am encouraged to believe that Mashonaland generally, and not only Charter District, is a hive of Native agricultural activity. One of the questions which the Lands Commission commended for consideration was, "Could the present method of occupying the land in Native Reserves be improved?" On the whole question of the potential value of Native Tribal agriculture and its promise for improvement, I would heartily recommend some of the remarks in a certain long article on Agriculture printed by a Phelps-Stokes Commission as part of their Report, published in 1925, which was entitled "Education in East Africa." It is an article contributed by a notable agricultural expert from the United States named Homer L. Shantz. It tends to clear the air about our Native African Agriculture. The Assistant Chief Native Commissioner of Southern Rhodesia has welcomed this article as useful reading for members of the Southern Rhodesian Native Department: "I want them all to read Shantz, as Native Agriculture is always being attacked." He went on to say: "The latest question is 'Should not Native Lands be stumped?' My feeling is if they are stumped will it not interfere with Nature's restorative process as outlined by Shantz?" I do not think that our own experienced Native Commissioner in Charter District has any doubt about the Natives being right from their point of view in this matter. On the other hand how plausible such a question seems to those with less experience of the land and of local conditions in Southern Rhodesia! The following words give a fair idea of the respect that Mr. Shantz tellingly inculcates with regard to the Native's traditional methods: "Without the scientific knowledge of methods of maintaining soil fertility and combating plant diseases, he has, by his method of rotating land, succeeded in avoiding both difficulties to a large extent. . . . In modern Agriculture there has been an unusually large amount of dogmatic teaching said to be based on scientific foundation. Deep-ploughing in a semi-arid country . . . increasing soil fertility or available nitrogen, when the water supply is inadequate—all these things have proved failures under certain conditions, although they are desirable under others. We have swung from one extreme to the other, and the 'slogans' of Agriculture must be questioned very seriously before they are allowed to interfere with the well-established customs of the Native."[1] ('Education in East Africa," page 370.)

As to Native Agriculture, Mr. H. L. Shantz, of the United States Department of Agriculture, shows a fullness of sympathy, as well as of knowledge, in the Paper he has contributed to this Educationalists' Report. Our own Southern Rhodesian Education Commission, which included no agricultural expert of Mr. Shantz's calibre, has dismissed the Native Agriculture of Mashonaland and Matabeleland with dogmatic disdain : "The agricultural methods are wasteful, slovenly and unnecessarily effective. . . ." Mr. Shantz, with fuller knowledge, speaks with fuller sympathy : "The agricultural methods of the Natives in Africa have often been condemned as shiftless, wasteful and destined to decrease the productivity of the country. Again, one meets continually the statement that the Native knows nothing about crop production. These statements, in a way, reflect the attitude of the European toward the Native, the assumption being that since he does not follow our methods and practices he must be essentially wrong. But there are many testimonies in the literature to the effect that the Native is an excellent agriculturist."

[1] Cf. Lord Reay's views (quoted in review of "The Forests of India," *Times Lit. Supplement*, Feb. 3rd, 1927) : "The more one looks into the various agricultural systems of various countries the more one becomes convinced that over-legislation in agricultural matters is a mistake, and that in the present condition of agricultural science, which is not by any means as far advanced as it ought to be, we must be careful to interfere as little as possible. . . . Local wants, local customs, and local systems of village tenure have a right not to be wantonly disturbed unless a very good cause be shown for it."

Mr. Shantz reminds us that it is well to bear in mind at the start that very little serious attention has been given to his methods and practices, and that there is no adequate scientific study of Native agriculture on which to base sound conclusions. He says there are "several practices which are quite uniformly condemned. . . . In general the Natives use excellent judgment in the selection of land and in the rotation of crops. . . . To advocate a change in the Native system until the Native is prepared to assume the added responsibility, or we are prepared and equipped to help him, would seem highly unjustifiable. It must not be presumed from the foregoing discussion that nothing can be done to improve Native agriculture.[1] However, before any changes are suggested, a thorough study should be made of the Native methods and only such changes suggested as are sure to bring beneficial results. The old foundation must not be destroyed until we are sure we can get along as well without it."

What has impressed me about Native Agriculture in the part of Mashonaland that has been my home for many years, has been not only the Natives' patient industry, but their adaptiveness to local climatic conditions. Mr. Shantz says of Africans' tillage: "In all cases Native agriculture is released from the tyranny of the plough, which so often forces the

[1] Undoubtedly a very strong case can be made out for the traditional Native Agriculture as a comparatively *perfect* and well-considered system for proceeding on the old lines. But with regard to the new problems raised by the introduction of ploughs, etc., the traditional Agriculture has no time-honoured experience to communicate. A. S. C.

cultivation of relatively poor level land and leaves the rich hillsides vacant."

I would like to ask three questions about Native and European agriculture in the District I know, which in the season 1924-1925 came through an extraordinarily wet summer and autumn. (1) Did Charter District Natives require or obtain any Government grain relief in the months that followed? (2) Did not these Natives trade surplus grain and ground-nuts on a very considerable scale? (3) How many bags of mealies or mealie meal (in some instances bought from local Natives) were doled out on Government terms (or ear-marked for doling out) in order to relieve the needs of that heir of all ages, the distressed European farmer, in the same District of Charter? I have heard myself that 200 bags of seed wheat for supplying local farmers were bought up by our Government in time for the sowing season [April-May, 1925].

Such a table as was given in the "S. Rhodesian Native Affairs Department Annual" of December, 1923, showing how work is divided between the men and the women in our part of Africa, may be found useful for dispelling cherished illusions or interested slanders as to Native agriculture being a mere woman's job. Evidence was given to the Land Commission of last year by a European recently arrived from work in the Transvaal Province with regard to the apparently favourable estimation that might be formed of cultivation in one part of Mashonaland (Manyikaland) as compared with cultivation by Natives further south. The coming of the plough would seem to have changed the Mashona's attitude towards those heavy red soil areas he was once accused of neglecting.

One notes a peculiarly wanton casting of a stone at the promise of an agricultural advance among local Africans. It is contained in the Report of the Imperial Government's East Africa Commission (1924-1925), which was not commissioned to report on the Southern Rhodesian Colony, but paid it a flying visit on its way to fulfil its proper functions in reporting about other African Territories. Comparatively ignorant as it was of African Agriculture in a Colony which it had no commission to investigate, it dogmatized about cotton, saying that " in some areas, particularly where irrigation is required or the rainfall is of short duration and in consequence continuous effort is required during a short period in the year " it is best grown as a European crop, " e.g., in Southern Rhodesia." What amount of personal investigation inspired such an uncalled-for statement ?

One great need of our Native cattle-country, as I view the economic outlook, is the establishment of a Canned Meat or Biltong Factory to buy up surplus Native cattle. As to proposed limitations of Native herds, I want to quote what the late Maurice Evans, C.M.G., says in a Report of his made to the Union Government : " The rearing of cattle is perhaps the most attractive occupation to the white man, and by tradition and taste, and also urged thereto by social customs, the native is at heart a cattle-lover and I think it would be very unfair if this opportunity in moderate degree were not given to him." If the sort of Factory I have indicated were established, and prospered, the Native breed of cattle might come into its own. As it is, they are comparatively healthy and hardy, strong and well adapted for subsisting on the sort of meagre pasturage that so much of the Native Reserve land[1] provides.

I go on to point out a second economic need of our more remote Native Areas, the need of that reasonable stimulus to productivity which some organized buying of Native grain and ground-nuts for cash may be expected to provide, if only the Government will offer a friendly hand of help. On this point I want to quote a high local authority as to our Colony—its produce and its marketing. He writes : " In the marketing of native crops: while at . . . I personally took the view that much could be done to encourage Native production of maize . . . ground-nuts, sunflower seeds, and now cotton, and this without detriment to European growers, in fact the very reverse. The greater the production in the country the better facilities for marketing.

"I have for a long time held the view that the officials of the Native Department might inculcate the spirit of co-operation into the Natives in the Reserves and encourage them to market their crops through a

[1] A comparison of the numbers of cattle lost through poverty of condition at the end of a dry season by Europeans and Natives respectively in the same neighbourhood may prove instructive. As to improvement of Native stock—a system by which spare bulls that local farmers are glad to sell are bought up by the Local Native Department, may not prove very satisfactory in its results. I have referred elsewhere to the care taken in Tanganyika Territory's Animal Husbandry activities " to preserve the natural hardiness of the breed."

headman or chief, who in turn with the assistance and/or advice of the Native Commissioner could market them through European co-operative organizations. We have now organizations of this kind at Victoria, Gwelo, Bulawayo, and Salisbury, and they are likely to spring up in other centres. The co-operative organization could be so organized as to make advances or make purchases, and possibly the Native Department could be drawn into it in some way also. This simply offers you a ground-work and you can elaborate it. . . . I am of opinion that after consideration something could be done on these lines." From what I have heard and seen of the Natives' enterprise in travelling to market their grain at a distance with sledges, or with those pack-donkeys which have become such a feature of our District in these last years; also their eagerness to realize in cash at short notice—hard-driven as they so often are to find money for Taxes and Dipping Dues—I should say that better facilities for disposal of produce might vastly increase our Native Areas' productivity. On a page of that Report to the Union Government which I have already quoted in this chapter, Maurice Evans says of the S.E. African Native : "If he could be assured of a minimum price at which all produce he offered would be bought it might be a great incentive to cultivation."

From an estimate given me by its Native Commissioner I am able to put the cultivation per head of Native adults (including grown boys and girls) in Charter District at approximately two acres.

Is the Native Small-holder to be sacrificed to the

fetish of "More Land for Settlers"? I should like to quote on this point a S. Rhodesian journalist writing in the year 1925:

"Now as to the Native as a small proprietor, I hold that our present policy of spending money on introducing white settlers and ignoring the native, who is and always must be the real base of the structure, is equivalent to standing the pyramid on its point, which will keep the white people busy running round to see that it does not fall over.[1] It certainly will fall over unless we can make the Native who constitutes nine-tenths[2] of the population into a good producing tax-paying citizen. How on earth can any sane man contemplate a State with nine-tenths of its population mere intelligent beasts of burden. The introduction of the white settler is a good thing, but side by side with his advent should come the development of the natural small-holder, the small tobacco and cotton producer, i.e., the native, who as he progresses should have his chance to become a peasant proprietor outside the Reserves, which will probably have to be maintained as communal centres for many years.

"Under present circumstances one-tenth[3] of the population holds over three-quarters[4] of the land, including practically all the best of it, and it is indefensible ethically speaking unless the white holder is willing to

[1] Cf. what Mrs. S. G. Millin says in "The South Africans": "In South Africa there is not plenty of room at the top, for the foundation is not strong enough to support a heavy upper storey, and yet, such room as there is, is high up."—A.S.C.

[2] 20/21 is a better approximate estimate, I should have said.—A.S.C.

[3] Should not one-tenth be rather one twenty-first?—A.S.C.

[4] Three-quarters?—A.S.C.

allow the progressive native his fair share. I maintain that the *State* cannot afford to distinguish *economically* between the native, who has attained a certain degree of civilization, and the white man."

We have heard much talk about educating the African in agricultural methods. A Report issued by the Phelps-Stokes Commission a few years ago remarked appositely: "It is evidently useless to train Natives in Agriculture if the land areas granted to them are too limited in size and too barren for profitable cultivation."

I would end this chapter of so many quotations with some lines of Mr. H. M. G. Jackson, a high official[1] in Southern Rhodesia's Native Department, who was lately one of those who enquired into the question of the Colony's Native Education. I have had occasion to comment unfavourably upon his Commission's ill-advised comment on our Native Agriculture. I would quote some lines of his that show a really fine spirit towards that African Question, whereof the African Agricultural and Educational Questions form an important part, but by no means the whole.

> "If we have faith to help the Slow Race onwards,
> And teach them freely all we know or learn;
> Awaken discontent divine within them
> Nor heed the hate that will within them burn
> —Nay, welcome it for sign of leaven working—
> When Freedom's birth tells them our aid to spurn;
> If we can check th' ungenerous fears that haunt us
> When they, our fledgelings, learn to fly alone,
> Why then we'll kneel to see Millennium dawning
> And Afric's joy for Afric's tears atone."

[1] Assistant Chief Native Commissioner.—A. S. C.

CHAPTER XII

LAMIA

CHAPTER XII

[" Modest as Keats was about his art, 'Lamia' is the one poem of which he speaks with praise. 'I am certain,' he says, 'that there is a fire in it, which must take hold of people in some way.'" WARTON LECTURE on Keats.

" Fool!" said the sophist in an undertone,
Gruff with contempt. . . ."

"Lamia" by JOHN KEATS.]

THE animus which Keats displayed against the interference of Apollonius, an interference dictated by what is called common-sense, has been deplored by his principal biographer.

When I turn over memories of my own, amassed within the last quarter of a century, I am disposed to contend that the poet's passionate resentment was to some extent justified. My own experience certifies me that Apollonius, well as he may have meant by his friend and former pupil, did in effect act towards him as a marplot and a busybody. Do I not know the tribe of Apollonius—I that have the honour of the acquaintance of so many local Apollonii?

People who affect to organize Native African Civilization, members of the flourishing firm of Augustus Wisdom & Co., with its many branches in British Africa, are, as I view them, scions of the great iconoclastic Apollonian gens.

For such infatuation as Apollonius of old denounced is apt to repeat itself under a southern sky, and the drama that was played in ancient Corinth is apt to get replayed in one's own down-south Colonial experiences. It is not my present concern to furnish any statistics as to how many present-day representatives of the rôle of Lycius there may be or may have been in modern South Africa beside myself. There need be no misgiving surely that the part of Lycius is likely to be too popular, or to be over-played, while those dominant influences in this part of the world—which I have already had occasion to describe—continue. What I am convinced of is my own vocation and election to play the part of Lycius myself, and to play it with unfeigned zest and impassioned sincerity. I am convinced that Fate has cast me for my welcome duty of playing this part. Why? Because I am, at least in some degree, awake to the charms and worth-while virtues of our Native African Life—a Life wherein I behold my own narrow but intense Vision of Beauty, in a word—Lamia. What wonder then if I should have a fellow-feeling for the poet who so passionately deprecated the outside interference of a marplot and a busybody—I who seek a happier outcome for my earthly relations with the Lamia of my own drama—happier than that which our prototypes were allowed to achieve—the Lycius and the Lamia whom the enlightened wisdom of friend Apollonius succeeded in reforming off the face of the earth.

Our first introduction to Lycius in Keats' poem is,

as may be remembered, to a Lycius charioteering "with calm uneager face." Near the outset of my time in Africa I might have rivalled my hero in his detachment, his calm and want of eagerness—so detached and cold were my own feelings about Africa. Placidly, with no particular complacency, used I to stride over Mashonaland, and to gaze upon its freakish quaintness. Unimpressed, I stared at the gargoyled grotesqueness of its granite country, so samely brown for so much of every year.

"Who ever lov'd that lov'd not at first sight?"

But perhaps I was not to love then because my Lamia of African Native Life was disguising her real charms in some dissembling unfamiliar form that baffled eyes so fresh from home.

Afterwards African Native Life shed any bizarre shape she may have worn to my outlandish eyes, and her appeal came home to me, and was revealed to me as Beauty.

I recognized that she had a finely simple shape, and that she wore time-honoured draperies.

My traditional view and outlook, far from challenging her approach to me like jealous sentries, surrendered me up to her on terms—Christian terms.

She came to me as a shepherdess might come, simply chatting, in her rusticity. I would have her told that the mighty Pan was kindly come to live with us below. I would have her tolerant of what that good news of His sojourn meant for all our world. Otherwise she taught, and I learned. Truth to tell, she seemed to have graces of Galilee, as well as those of Arcadia. She was happy-go-lucky about food, yet she throve on it—like the grey-blue doves of her own rocks. Her flowery, careless mood took small thought for her raiment.

I have watched her, year in, year out, hoeing laboriously at deep trenches and pits for her root and rice gardens, weeding multitudinous weed-choked furrows in our bounteous rain-times, reaping millet over wide acres with a meagre knife-blade, winnowing on strown rock-floors—the gold-green of the spindrift blowing about her—on gusty days. The shapes and patterned colours of her water-jars please me: so does the queen's poise of the head that carries them, so does the patient persistence of her goings to-and-fro, sundown after sundown, season after season. She works at her own yoked beasts' pace, by suntime, and in her own seasons. She does not fluctuate idly without term or scope; she does not half live a hundred different lives! I do not find her idle, whatsoever these well-salaried and cold-eyed Kulturists of Messrs. Wisdom & Co. may have to say. That somewhat exotic pioneer our European farmer—is he not glad now and then to buy maize-corn from her rather than to grow it on his own farm?

Some of our High-Priests and High-Deacons want to hustle her, do they? I would have her move herself towards this World's Light; but I would avert the contagion of their hustling ways from her. Is it not a moot point whether some of them have much in common with the Light, I mean the Light that the Gospel and our own hearts proclaim?

May our "mighty Pan," bless her and secure her room to plough, and keep her crops from her own weather-harms, and her cattle from our imported cattle's murrains !

How painstaking are the Apollonians in their endeavour to convince me of the incalculable and serpentine nature of this Lamia, this African Life—that I take at her face value ! They arraign as utterly indefensible the character of that attachment, which I —a modern—have formed for her—an ancient. They have many a warning to impress upon me as to the infinitely variegated differentiations of Africa's point of view from our own.

> "Striped like a zebra, freckled like a pard."

Yes, doubtless she is all that—this "Gordian shape of dazzling hue." I thank God that she is what she is. I allow her lithe plasticity to be serpentine, if you will have it so. But I am encouraged by remembering Who it was that claimed a Serpent [Brazen, Passant on a Cross' Banner-Pole] as His own heraldic cognizance.

Is she commercially unsound ? At any rate she seems to me to do most of the rough work of our Territory, and also to grow the bulk of her own food somehow—having in good years much to spare for sale besides, and she breeds astonishingly few paupers. Hers is a fairish way of prospering, so it seems to my poor judgment. If only they would leave her enough land, and not wallow in land-lust as they do so nakedly !

What? Is she drunken, rankly animistic, detrimentally superstitious, prone to nameless earthiness? Well, let those who are free from whisky-fever, who have no séances, and automatic scripts, and contraceptives, and facilities for unlocking wedlock, in their own lands—be the first to level stones at her! "A childish devotee" am I? If you mean that I am devoted to a childish Race, please believe in my impenitence. It takes all Races—childish Races as well as jaded Nations—to make up the commonwealth of a workaday world. As to the childish having nothing to teach the staled, Christ, who prescribed the terms of our conversion's acceptability, has His own immutable view on that matter.

I believe in the racial worth of Native Africa, and I long to see that racial worth given its chance, even in this present stage of our racialized earth, when it "sometimes seems as if the West, like some enormous Saurian, some alligator of antediluvian magnitude had fixed its gaze upon the coloured civilizations in various parts of Africa and the East, till its slow brain gradually rose to the conception that it was hungry and they were good to eat. Then the great masticators set to their work."[1]

Until the present tyranny of Anglo-Dutch Racialism be overpast I would have Native Africa set comparatively free in Native Areas allotted more amply than in our discreditable past—sanctuaries made safer than of old from European intrusions.

I have one word of counsel for this Native African

[1] Professor Gilbert Murray's "Essays and Addresses," p. 193.

Life—this Lamia, that has so endeared herself to me. It is to beware of her Apollonii, of those Europeans or Americans, be they Churchmen or Statesmen, philanthropists or exploitationists—who have no faith[1] in her own indigenous, unexploited destiny, and who would presume to undermine others' faith in it.

> " But fly our paths, our feverish contact fly !
> For strong the infection of our mental strife,
> Which, though it gives no bliss, yet spoils for rest ;
> And we should win thee from thy own fair life,
> Like us distracted, and like us unblest.
> Soon, soon thy cheer would die,
> Thy hopes grow timorous, and unfix'd thy powers,
> And thy clear aims be cross and shifting made ;
> And then thy glad perennial Youth would fade,
> Fade, and grow old at last, and die like ours."

[1] What amounts to a deplorable confession of unfaith in Native Africa is to be found in that widely circulated treatise, " Education in East Africa " [Phelps Stokes Commission Report, 1925]. I gratefully acknowledge that the compilation contains much which every friend of Africa ought to appreciate, and that Dr. Jesse Jones has worked nobly for Christian peace and goodwill in African territories. Nevertheless one sentence as to native schools in Southern Rhodesia seems to me symptomatic of a perniciously faithless tendency in his general educational outlook. " Justice to the education of the natives requires that the number of pupils in the first and second class schools shall be regarded as the real measure of school provision." In *The Bulawayo Chronicle's* leading article on the report (June 6, 1925) may be found a criticism of singular discernment—" A visit is mentioned to one of the third-class schools. . . . Had the Commission tested the education actually given by the poorly qualified native teacher with so little equipment they would have been surprised." The *Chronicle* went on to say that the wonder, in its estimation, was that in the circumstances so much was " done and so much accomplished." Two veteran Mashonaland backveld missionaries, Canon and Mrs. Lloyd, have written of " what are called third-class schools, whether receiving a Government grant or not." " They are very important social centres. The village school is the hub of the little world of the natives around it, and from it, imperfect as it may be, come those influences which do battle against heathen superstitions, ignorance and drinking habits. They are exceedingly popular among natives. In the local management of church and school the native is finding a new sphere of interest and an opportunity of accepting and shouldering responsibility. These schools are helping to rural and social content and so have a political value in these unsettled times " (see 1924 Missionary Conference Proceedings, pages 25 and 26).

Arguably, the veld school, though it may be a poor thing, is in a far more real sense the native African's own than those predominantly European (or American) institutions—schools of the first and second class. One aspect of a veld school-church may surely have been ignored too often. It is a humble shrine, but it proudly enshrines native Africa's sacred right to a certain measure of self-expression and a certain amount of freedom in self-development. I speak as one who has seen much of many African villages. A policy of encouraging those whom it is desired to improve to improve themselves has a lot to be said for it in Native Africa. Charles Kingsley's parable in "The Water Babies" has useful lessons to teach the would-be reformers of ancient Africa to-day. Tom, when he went in search of Mother Carey, "expected, of course—like some grown people who ought to know better—to find her snipping, piecing, fitting, stitching, cobbling, basting, filing, planing, hammering, turning, polishing, moulding, measuring, chiselling, clipping, and so forth, as men do when they go to work to make anything. But instead of that, she sat quite still. . . . 'I am never more busy than I am now,' she said, without stirring a finger. 'I heard, ma'am, that you were always making new beasts out of old.' 'So people fancy. But I am not going to trouble myself to make things, my little dear. I sit here and make them make themselves.' 'You are a clever fairy, indeed,' thought Tom. And he was quite right." Too few, alas! in the Africa of our day are out for encouragement rather than interference. A. S. C.

POSTSCRIPT.

["Now as ever helplessness breeds tyranny"
EDWIN SMITH.]

I append some Notes received from a Philo-African who attended a recent Rhodesia Agricultural Union Conference as a farmers' representative. He tells me that he feels that to have the Native Commissioners stuck down in the Reserves means a further curtailment of the little bit of freedom the Natives have got. He says, writing on April 10th, 1927: "Unless crime is clearly on the increase (so far as I know there is no proof of this) why all this fuss and bother?" Why, indeed? Surely in responsibly-governed Rhodesia one of the gravest perils is the tendency of Europeans "clothed in a little brief authority" to insist on treating the Native Areas as happy playgrounds for the British red-tape regulator.

NOTES ON R. A. U. CONFERENCE, APRIL 4TH AND 5TH.

The Conference met to consider a report by its Committee on Native Labour.

I.

The first paragraph contended that the natives on the Reserves were undisciplined, out of control, and given to much beer-drinking. The authority of the Chief was gone, and the Conference proposed that the Native Commissioners should be stationed on the Reserves to supply the place of the defunct Chief. One speaker declared that this first paragraph was a declaration of the utter failure of the past policy both of the British South Africa Company and the new Government. Another said that Native Commissioners were out of touch with the natives, and ignorant of what was going on.

I protested that the whole paragraph was based on an assumption for which not an atom of evidence had been produced.

If the Government's native policy was so faulty then all the laudatory things that had been said about it by High Commissioners and others in authority were away from the truth. This is not the common opinion held about it.

I said that with the increase of administrative work it was a physical impossibility for Native Commissioners to be in touch with the natives as they were in the early days. But that they were out of touch with the people and ignorant of what was going on was contrary to my experience.

Now they proposed to make this new Official stationed on the Reserve a Sanitary Inspector, a School Supervisor, a Controller of Beer Brewing, and general bosser-up. This would fetter him in the exercise of his judicial functions. I said that it was hardly fair to men who had entered the Service expecting to fulfil the duties of a Magistrate to put them to a job like this. I doubted whether this kind of position would attract men of education and culture as at present. If you want to assist the people on the Reserves I said, then there are other ways of doing it. A layman with sympathy and "nous" might do useful work and leave the Native Commissioners free, as at present, to exercise their judicial functions.

II.

Taxation for a "Reserve Betterment Fund."

The maximum amount to be levied for this Fund was not to exceed 30s. for each tax-paying native. One speaker declared that to procure this money the native would have to go out to work.

I moved, as an amendment, that when the Government instituted Native Councils in the Reserves, these Councils should be empowered and encouraged to tax themselves for their own betterment purposes. I protested against this arbitrary increase of taxation. My amendment was lost.

III.

A Gag on Missionaries.

It would seem that strong exception was taken to my address at the Missionary Conference, and it was affirmed that the Government was the one and only Trustee of the natives.

I protested that we had the right, as Englishmen, to express our views on matters affecting the native people. We have not in the past nor do we now wish to assume plenary powers. But if injustice is being done,[1] we have the right to protest, and likewise to express our views on all political proposals affecting these politically dumb people. We endeavour to expound the implications of the Gospel for the practical affairs of the native people, and likewise to urge that they have fair play from their white governors. This was the attitude I had always taken up, and, whatever the R.A.U. might say or do, I should not alter my course of action.[2]

John McChlery and a few others supported me. A Resolution that this Clause be deleted was lost by 25 to 53 votes.

IV.

The control of education should be vested in the Native Commissioner, who shall consult with the Education Department and Native Chiefs.

I said that the view of the Missionaries as expressed in the recent Conference was that Education should be controlled by the Education Department. No objection was raised to Magistrates visiting our schools, but that we should be responsible to the Education Department alone.

[1] As one of the best friends of Africans and Missionaries in Mashonaland, that gallant pioneer, Robert Duncan, phrased it: " We don't want to fight, but we won't run away."—A.S.C.

[2] Cf. Lord Olivier in his Preface to " Smith of Demerara," (1923) " It is therefore, I believe, still essential—however well disposed and enlightened the Colonial Office, the Mandates Commission of the League of Nations, Colonial Governors and officials, and white colonists themselves may be— essential in the interest of sound civilisation in the undeveloped parts of the world in whose government we have intervened, that there should be a continual supply of missionaries, entirely independent of any secular association with the governments of those territories and as independent as possible of the patronage of the dominant white congregations."—A.S.C.

V.

Punishment of Crime.

It was assumed that ordinary imprisonment was not regarded by the native as either a slur or a hardship. Spare diet, solitary confinement, and caning of first offenders was recommended.[1]

I gave instances where natives were prepared to borrow money on almost any terms to avoid gaol for themselves or their friends. My experience was that they really loathed it. Against the caning I uttered a most emphatic protest. In my view, flogging was a return to barbarism : it brutalized those who inflicted it, and brutalized those on whom it was imposed.[2]

John McChlery joined in my protest. We were as voices crying in the wilderness. The Clause passed almost unanimously.

These were the Clauses in which I was mainly against the R.A.U.'s recommendations. Others were on much better lines. The outstanding impression was one of deep disappointment. Had the mood of this Conference been different I was going to propose that a round-table Conference be instituted, at which all interests and the natives be represented to talk over the whole question, but this was impossible.

[1] Appetite comes with eating. It would seem that, encouraged by the Dominions Office's uneasy approval of the Native Juvenile Apprenticeship Act, the S. Rhodesian Government has already drafted a Bill for extending the powers of Native Commissioners (a provision for the caning of Juveniles being expressly included). A.S.C.

[2] One who knows has told me : " The nickname by which the Germans were commonly known in their part of East Africa at the time of the War was ' Watu wa Hamstashara ' ; that is, ' The People of the Fifteen '—that is, lashes."—A.S.C.

Note by A. S. C.—Why are the farmers, or so many of them, agitating about tightening the European pressure on Native Reserves? Obviously because they want more cheap Native labourers. But there is *no* unlimited supply of indigenous Native labourers—only about 210,000 at an estimate. The S. Rhodesian Minister of Agriculture[1] said, on March 30th, 1927: "Naturally the whole of those natives could not come out to work for the European employer, leaving some 600,000 women and children and old men in the reserves to look after themselves."

When the Census of 1926 was taken, from 75,000 to 80,000 were shown to be out in service.

Attempts by Europeans to stampede their Legislative Assembly into catch-vote interference with African Areas point a clear moral: it is that Native Interests ought to be effectively represented in that Assembly—for the present by nominated European Members, these Members being nominees of our Home Government, or of our Governor. The Preface to this book stresses a real and an urgent need—the representation of hard-pressed Native interests in a Colony where one-twentieth of the population has so much to say as to its law-making, and nineteen-twentieths so little.

[1] The Hon. J. W. Downie.

APPENDIX

A SEGREGATION AREAS SCHEME-IN-BEING FOR SOUTHERN RHODESIA

["Those who have used to cramp liberty have gone so far as to resent even the liberty of complaining; although a man upon the rack was never known to be refused the liberty of roaring as loud as he thought fit."—DEAN SWIFT.]

CHAPTER I

A SEGREGATION POLICY OBTAINS A BRITISH COMMISSION'S SUPPORT

CHAPTER I

[" Granted that the division was fairly made, such a measure would have the advantage of giving security to both communities against encroachment by the other."—J. H. OLDHAM.]

THE Report of a Commission, appointed by the Governor of Southern Rhodesia, Sir John Chancellor, was made public in February, 1926. This Commission consisted of Sir William Morris Carter, ex-Chief Justice in Tanganyika Territory, who acted as Chairman, and of two Southern Rhodesian Heads of Departments (the Chief Native Commissioner, [Sir Herbert Taylor], and Mr. W. J. Atherstone, Surveyor-General and Director of Lands). Their Commission's Terms of Reference were these : " (1) To inquire into and report upon the expediency and practicability of setting apart defined areas outside the boundaries of the Native Reserves, (*a*) within which Natives only shall be permitted to acquire ownership of or interest in land, and (*b*) within which only Europeans shall be permitted to acquire ownership of or interest in land; and (2) Should the Commission consider that the above proposal is expedient and practicable ; to report generally as to the manner in which effect should be given to such policy and the steps necessary to carry it out; and, further, to indicate any areas in which it seems desirable in the light of present conditions that early action should be taken with a view to limiting the rights of acquisition to Natives or Europeans."

The Commission gives us a historical sketch of the position of Natives with regard to Land in Southern Rhodesia. It may suffice us here to take up the story at the time when the bulk of those Recommendations which had been made by a Native Reserves Commission (constituted in May, 1914) "were embodied in the Order in Council, 1920, in which certain defined lands known as Native Reserves, are vested in the High Commissioner, and set apart for the sole and exclusive use and occupation of the Native inhabitants of Southern Rhodesia." The Commission remarks that although "this Order in Council gave finality to the matter of Native Reserves, it in no way affected the legal rights of the individual Natives to acquire land secured to them under the Order in Council of 1898," by which "a Native may acquire, hold, encumber, and dispose of land on the same conditions as a person who is not a Native. . . ."

But the Chief Native Commissioner in his Reports of 1919 and 1920, "advocated the reservation of land, where possible contiguous to existing Reserves, for acquisition by individual Natives, and instanced, as illustrative of the real desire of Natives to acquire land, that several of them had purchased land." Then followed the events that have been sketched in the Introduction. An important covering despatch from Mr. Churchill as Colonial Secretary (associated with that Scheme for Responsible Government which had the approval of the Colonial Office) was published in a Southern Rhodesian Government Gazette Extraordinary of January 19th, 1922, and dealt with a request made by a delegation sent from Southern Rhodesia to London—" that specific districts should be set aside by the High Commissioner in which Natives alone might acquire land and within which Europeans should not be allowed to do so."

The Colonial Secretary wrote sympathetically as we have seen : " I have informed the delegates that the existing clause enshrines a long accepted principle, and that I should be unwilling to an alteration, the corollary of which seems to be the exclusion of Natives from other areas; but that if full and impartial inquiry should show, after Responsible Government had come into force, that some amendment of the law is necessary, His Majesty's Government would be prepared to consider an amendment."

On the 30th May, 1924, His Excellency the Governor, in his speech at the opening of the Southern Rhodesian Legislative Assembly, said : " I propose accordingly to appoint a Commission to inquire into and report upon the whole subject." (The Chairman of this proposed Commission, so the Report tells us, was appointed by the Secretary of State.) The Commission was duly constituted in January, 1925, with the Terms of Reference that we have quoted. In reviewing the position in Southern Rhodesia, the Commission states that under " the existing law, outside the Reserves, Natives and Europeans have the same rights as regards the acquisition and holding of land, consequently there is nothing in law to prevent Natives from acquiring land among Europeans throughout the Colony, or Europeans acquiring land in areas which are thickly populated by Natives."

The Commission goes on to tell us that the " evidence which has been given before the Commission leaves no room for doubt as to the wishes of all classes of the inhabitants of Southern Rhodesia who are affected; and we have no hesitation in finding that an overwhelming majority of those who understand the question are in favour of the existing law being amended, and of the establishment of separate areas in which each of the two races, black and white, respectively, should be permitted to acquire interests in land. Missionaries, farmers and town dwellers, the officials of the Native Department, the Natives[1] in the out-districts and Reserves, in so far as they can grasp the subject, and the more advanced Natives are, generally speaking, all of one mind in this respect."

The Commission proceeds to give the point of view of the farmer, the Native, the Missionary, the Official of the Native Department, and of town-dwellers, European and Native, so far as it has been enabled to arrive at and to summarize their very various points of view.

(i) " The farmer considers that his stock and produce will be endangered by the proximity of Native

[1] This argument from these Natives' own preference would have a more genuine sound if the Commission were not proposing to ride rough-shod over their traditional form of land-tenure in such Purchase Areas as it proposes to offer them.—A.S.C.

land-holders, whose less progressive and careless methods will spread disease amongst his crops and cattle; in many cases he suspects the honesty of the Native, and fears that his crops and implements will be stolen; and he objects from social reasons to the Native as a neighbour; moreover, he has no doubt that his land will depreciate in value if a Native buys a neighbouring farm."

(ii) "The Native, on the other hand, prefers to live among his own people, and has no wish to acquire land among white people if he can obtain suitable land elsewhere; he dreads the trouble which arises from the white man not understanding him, and the worry to which he is subjected by the impounding of his straying flocks and herds, with the consequent expense he is put to in releasing them from the pound; in many cases he realizes the growing difficulty of obtaining land in competition with the whites."

(iii) "The missionary is more guarded in the expression of his opinion, as he was unwilling on behalf of the Native to surrender the rights of which the Native is in possession; but in the existing state of opinion, both black and white, he is satisfied that the interests of the Native would be better served if he is enabled to acquire suitable land in sufficient quantities among his own people and apart from the whites, where he will have a better opportunity of progressing in his own sphere along lines more suited to his race."

(iv) We are told that this last view is also "held by the Official of the Native Department, who also feels that the proper administration of the Natives will be facilitated by the adoption of the policy of separate areas."

(v) " The white town-dweller is averse from having a Native as his neighbour, whether as a resident or as a competitor in his profession, trade or craft."

(vi) On the other hand, the Commission assures us that " the Native town-dweller at present is only anxious to obtain a place where he can reside in comfort with his family, if he has one, and, if he wishes to trade, to have some opportunity of setting up a shop or practising his craft."

The Commission warns us, after it has laid before us in order these contrasted views, that in " the world generally the relationships between the white and coloured races tend to become more and more embittered; and of those who have given the subject most thought, many fear that wars of extermination between the races will take place in the future unless every effort is made to secure a better understanding between them." Mr. J. H. Oldham is quoted by the Commission as noting in his " Christianity and the Race Problem," that the best minds seem to be turning to racial and social segregation on the basis of equality of opportunity as the solution. Mr. Oldham in his book asks, " Is this a desirable solution and is it practicable ? " He answers his own question by saying : " Segregation may not, indeed cannot, be the ultimate ideal. But at a particular stage in the development of the human race it may be the arrangement which, on the whole, makes for harmony and peaceful progress."

Speaking of other writers as well as Mr. Oldham the Commission says : " All these writers emphasize the growing seriousness of the race problem and the importance of the land question in relation to it, and their writings show that the desire of both races in Southern Rhodesia for segregation with regard to the holding of land is no mere passing phase of local feeling, but that it is in accordance with a policy which is growing in favour in the world generally, and which is coming to be regarded more and more as the only practicable solution at the present time of the problem of the inter-relations of black and white."

The Commission proceeds to pronounce judgment as to the expediency of separate Areas for the European and African Races in His Majesty's Colony of Southern Rhodesia :

" In view therefore, of the state of opinion of both races in this country, which we think is unlikely to be materially changed for many years, if at all, and which coincides with the accepted policy in the Union of South Africa, its neighbour to the south, and of the difficulties which arise throughout the world in countries where the population is composed of different coloured races, each in considerable number; we are of opinion that it is expedient that separate areas for the holding of land should be set aside for the two races."

We may well bring this chapter to an end with the Land Commission Report's solemn words on Racial prejudice as it has been found to exist in present-day Africa : " From whatever cause it arises, whether instinctive or acquired, there can be no question as to the existence at the present day of certain prejudices between the white and the black races wherever these races are each living in considerable numbers in the same country; they are prejudices which are not entertained in Europe to any comparable extent, owing to the preponderance of the white peoples; but in Africa they cannot be ignored or belittled, however unfortunate they may be; and the question of how they can be overcome can, without doubt, be better decided if the opportunities for friction between the two races are reduced to the minimum compatible with the increased co-operation between them in developing the resources of the country which is both inevitable and desirable."

M

CHAPTER II

THE BRITISH COMMISSION ADVANCES CERTAIN PROPOSALS FOR GIVING THAT POLICY PRACTICAL EFFECT

CHAPTER II

[" Is not the whole land before thee? Separate thyself, I pray thee, from me; if thou wilt take the left hand, then I will go to the right; or if thou depart to the right hand, then I will go to the left . . . and Lot journeyed east; and they separated themselves the one from the other."—GENESIS xiii.]

"WE now come," say the Commissioners, " to a consideration of the second main question into which we have to inquire—the practicability of setting apart separate areas for each race."

The Commission proposes to leave over 17 million acres for future consideration. They comprise back-blocks of country in the North, North-West, West, and South-East of Southern Rhodesia. " They will later provide opportunities for land acquisition not only for the Natives residing in or near and for Europeans, but also for minimizing the effect of any miscalculations which time may show to have been made by us in our proposed apportionment of land between the two races."

The Commission tells us that in dividing up the Territory about 31 millions of acres that have been alienated to Europeans and more than 21 millions of acres that have been set apart as Reserves for Natives are not available. Out of the balance of over 43 millions of acres which are available, these 17 millions of acres in remote parts that we have referred to are reserved for future determination. The Commission says: "Although a considerable portion of the land available under existing conditions is unsuitable at present for the requirements of either the white or black population, yet a large proportion of it is suitable, and we consider that the setting apart of separate areas is a practicable proposition at the present time, and that Southern Rhodesia is in a very fortunate position compared with the Union of South Africa in being able to give effect to a policy which the bulk of its inhabitants so clearly desire. With a firm determination to do justice; and the expenditure of a moderate sum of money in expropriation, in our opinion the whole of that part of the Colony in which a conflict of interests between the black and white is likely to arise for several years to come can be divided into separate areas for the two races, with a minimum of disturbance of existing rights, and to the great advantage of the future welfare of the country."

What may be called, humanly speaking, Native Rhodesia's Now-or-Never opportunity has arrived according to these Commissioners, whose eyes are not only on the present but the future—"Certain difficulties arise even now in providing for the legitimate requirements of the Natives, and as each year goes by the problem will be of increasing difficulty, as Europeans take up more and more of the land which may be properly required for the present, and more especially for the future, needs of the Native. To our minds, therefore, if the policy of separate areas is to be adopted the present is the time for its adoption; otherwise the conditions are likely to become such that the setting apart of suitable areas will involve such an expenditure of capital and such a disturbance of existing rights as to make it impracticable."

The Commission shows clearly that the decision as to proportions and percentages of land, amplitude and acceptability of areas, and so on has a clear moral bearing. It says, and I make no apology for giving here Paragraphs 74-77 word for word:

74. "In one sense, and that a most vital one, the practicability of the policy depends, as we have already indicated, upon a determination to do justice, which involves willingness of the members of the Legislative Assembly on behalf of the voters of the country to support legislation which will ensure a fair proportion of land being set apart for Native acquisition."

75. "In law, as we have said, each of the two races has at present the same rights as to the acquisition of land outside the Native Reserves, and any alteration of the law in the direction of limiting the rights of acquisition of land to certain areas for the one race, and to certain other areas for the other race obviously necessitates the relinquishment by each race of something—the right to acquire land anywhere in the Colony."

76. "The desire of the whole population, black and white, who are interested in and understand the question is, generally speaking, in favour of separate

areas, but it is in fact the white element of the population which originally asked for an amendment of the law in this direction, and it depends upon votes of members of the Legislative Assembly, who, to all intents and purposes, have been elected by that portion of the Community, whether any alteration of that law should take place; it is for them to determine to what extent they are willing to surrender their rights in order to obtain the benefits which the policy of separate areas will bring to the white community."

77. "Unless they are prepared to surrender these rights to an extent which is considered by the Government of the Colony and the Imperial Government to be fair and equitable to both Natives and Europeans, presumably no alteration in the Constitution will come into being."

How then does the Commission propose to divide those parts of the Colony that seem to menace avoidable friction, if they be not soon divided?

The Commission as a whole[1] recommends that the Natives be allotted over six million acres in Purchase Areas, and that over eighty thousand acres be regarded as semi-Neutral[2] Areas for purchase, so that over 17

[1] Sir Morris Carter and Sir Herbert Taylor recommend certain further augmentations of the Natives' share of the Division, from which their colleague dissents. They recommend over a million acres in Neutral Areas, and an addition of 117 thousand acres of Native Purchase Areas.

[2] See paragraph 162 for definition of semi-Neutral Areas. The Commission says "it is advisable that such holdings should ultimately form part of those Native Areas." It is speaking of European holdings which form an entrant angle in recommended Native Purchase Areas. The Commission considers, however, that it is unnecessary that "the expense of expropriation" should be undertaken in these cases.

million acres would still be left as available for alienation to Europeans.

The Commission calculates that the European Area represents approximately 62 per cent. of the total area dealt with, and the Native area represents approximately 37 per cent. of that area.

Before proceeding to briefly review the Commission's proposals I would draw attention to the estimates of indigenous Native Population in Mashonaland and Matabeleland which the Report itself gives. They amount to 813,947 Natives for the two Provinces. That European population, to which it is proposed to allot 62 per cent.[1] of the ground now to be divided may be estimated as about 38,200 souls in all.

[1] Paragraph 208 in the Report gives a resumé of how this figure is arrived at: "It will be seen that if the above recommendations are adopted the European areas will amount in all to 48,605,898 acres, comprising land which is alienated to them at present, and the Urban Areas, land which is at present Crown land, and 32,875 acres which are at present alienated to Natives; and the Native Areas will total 28,933,362 acres, comprising the Reserves, land which is at present Crown Land, land which is at present alienated to Europeans, totalling 473,915 acres, land which is now in Native possession, totalling 11,646 acres, and the lands held by Missions, which may be regarded as held in the interests of the Native, and the larger part of which the Native is permitted to live upon or cultivate, even if he may not have more permanent interest therein."

CHAPTER III

THE NATIVE LAND-PURCHASER'S "QUID PRO QUO"

(i) A Summary

CHAPTER III

[" Your hand ; a covenant : We will have these things set down by lawful counsel, and straight away for Britain ; lest the bargain should catch cold, and starve ; I will fetch my gold, and have our two wagers recorded."—SHAKESPEARE—" Cymbeline," Act 1, Scene 5.]

[" Sir, you are 1½ million, we are 5 million. Nevertheless, we are willing to divide on President Kruger's plan. You divide the country and we will pick, or we will divide and you shall pick."—S. Plaatje at the Official Native Conference, Pretoria, 1926.]

THE Commission gives some idea of the difficulty that may arise through the need of obtaining hearty co-operation from representatives of a white community of oligarchs in a small "self-governing" British Colony, if any sort of equitable segregation Areas Scheme is to be approved :

" It will be only natural that a fair and equitable apportionment of land in the Colony will seem to many Europeans a generous and perhaps over-generous provision for the Native." The Commission notices the diversity of opinion in the evidence it has received as to the amount of land which ought to be set aside for each Race. " On the one hand, the view has been expressed that, in their Reserves, the Natives have already more land than should have been allowed them; on the other, it is considered that 60 per cent. of the available land should be set aside for acquisition by them. The two paragraphs that follow these words are given in full.

80. "A very large number of witnesses have declined to express any opinion upon the subject, but of those who have done so it may be said that the majority of Europeans, apart from Missionaries and Officials in the Native Administrations, have expressed the view that less, rather than more, than a quarter of the available land should be allocated for individual acquisition by Natives; though one or two of such witnesses have considered that half of such land would not be too much."

81. "The majority of the Natives who have expressed an opinion upon the subject, and of the Missionaries who have spoken for them, consider that the land should be divided equally; though a few Missionaries have thought that less than that proportion might suffice the Native; one of them considered that a third might be enough."

A subsequent paragraph is very important as expounding the momentous issues that the advocates of the Natives' cause in Southern Rhodesia have been faced with in taking the line they have taken as to a Segregation Areas division of land.

84. "The advocates of the Native cause were naturally reluctant to ask for a policy which may be regarded as involving the surrender by the Native of rights which he already possesses and of setting up a differentiation between him and the white man, which at present does not in law exist. They felt that the Native would be giving up the potential

right to be the owner of all the land in the Colony, and did not wish to do anything which would benefit the present generation at the expense of posterity. They have deliberated the question with much anxiety, and have decided in favour of the policy of separate areas after carefully weighing all the advantages and disadvantages, and they advocate that policy, subject to the proviso that an adequate provision of suitable land is made. We are disposed to think that in their desire to do justice to the Native they are inclined to stress the disparity in numbers between the two races, and to over-estimate the value of the rights of the Native to acquire land anywhere in the Colony."

In support of their view the Commission calls attention to the fact that Europeans have acquired 31 million acres, Natives have only purchased 45 thousand acres so far in Southern Rhodesia.

The Commission admits that it is true that most of the Natives probably have not been aware of their rights as to land-purchase, but declares it to be equally true that they "have not had the means to acquire large areas by purchase. Such means as they possess consist of cattle, which they are averse from selling; they regard them as their sole wealth and as an index of position, and as a necessity for the obtaining of wives. Their cattle are increasing rapidly, and other means are coming to them, in the form of wages, and from the sale of produce, so that their ability to purchase will doubtless gradually increase, but it will be many years to come before they can compete with the white man on terms of equality: meanwhile, if nothing is done, all the most desirable land will be in possession of the latter, and it will only be by the payment of such price as the white man demands that the Native will be able to secure land. If the European is successful as a settler in this country, that price will in any event be high; but in addition, unless a very marked change in opinion takes place the Europeans will not in most cases be willing to sell to a Native, who, although he may be in possession of the means to purchase, will have great difficulty in finding a willing seller of land in suitable localities."

The Commission has already noted the fact that no land appears to have been sold to Natives by the Chartered Company or by the Government (one farm only, we believe, has been leased to Natives), "and has drawn the conclusion that although an appreciable amount has been purchased from private owners, it would seem doubtful how far an application from a Native for the purchase of Crown land would be entertained; and if this be so, the Native in practice has no opportunity of purchasing land from the Crown, and has to pay an enhanced price in purchasing from a private owner." The Commission now goes on to indicate the considerable difficulty the would-be land-purchaser, if he be a Native, may find in seeking to purchase the land of a private European owner. The Commission mentions "the almost unanimous statements of European land-holders to the effect that they did not think that a European should have the right to sell to Natives, and of their freedom from objection to being deprived of that right in the event of separate areas being established. A missionary in the course of conversation, informed us of a case in which one of his European friends, who was remaining in the country, refused an offer made by Natives to purchase his land." He accepted an offer a good deal lower made by a European. "The missionary, in making this statement, was illustrating the difficulty of the Native in obtaining land by purchase; he was not expressing concurrence with the action of his friend."

The Commission concludes that in "such circumstances the right of the Native to purchase land anywhere in the Colony appears to us to be less valuable than might at first sight appear to be the case."

It moreover endeavours to console those who are oppressed by the huge responsibility of helping to support a decision which barters away the Native's right to purchase anywhere under the existing law—"Further, in the event of the European not being successful or ceasing to regard Southern Rhodesia as a White man's country, we apprehend that he will be anxious to secure purchasers of his land, and will cast his vote in favour of the law being again amended, and of the white areas, in whole or in part, being again thrown open to purchase by Natives."

Having made some show of easing the burdened consciences of those of us who are disposed in its opinion to magnify the Native's right to a *quid pro quo* (should the law be altered), the Commission goes on to impress upon possible European dissentients the case for making the Native Land-Purchaser's *quid pro quo* a really substantial one, if the Native's present right is to be bought out with the Imperial Government's approval. "On the other hand, many Europeans, although desirous that the Native should be prevented from acquiring land in their midst, do not appear to have fully realized the fact that the Native has in law the same rights to acquire land as they have, and that when the Reserves were set aside there was no intention whatever of depriving him of that right, and that if he gives up the right to acquire land anywhere he must secure in return a real *quid pro quo*."

. . . . . .

Certain considerations that it would be well for certain Europeans to bear in mind before they dismiss any substantial provision of Native Purchase Areas as ridiculous and unnecessary, are advanced by the Report:

"Nor do Europeans seem to have fully appreciated the extent to which in their own time, and still more in that of their children, such acquisition is certain to take place. Even now some Europeans have found Natives coming in as their neighbours, although the Native has not as yet more than begun to be aware of his rights. When he fully realizes them, the desire to purchase land will increase to an extent which is not contemplated by many people. Moreover, Europeans who have decided to leave the country, or who are in financial difficulties, will frequently not refrain from selling their land to Natives, however much they are in agreement as to the undesirability of having Natives as neighbouring land owners. Those who remain will then not only be neighboured by persons whom they consider undesirable, but will also be faced with the fact that their own property has depreciated in selling value by such contiguity. . . . Others feel that there is a crying need for greatly increased European settlement in the country, and think that if relatively large areas are set aside for Native acquisition there will not be land available. Upon this point we consider there is no ground for fear; our duties have necessitated extensive travelling throughout the Colony, and one cannot fail to be impressed with the vast areas which are calling for settlement." With regard to a proposition made by the Executive Council of the Rhodesia Agricultural Union urging *that not more than one million acres should be at present set aside for Native use, but that the Policy of separate Areas should be established*, the Commission is decisively and commendably clear :

" If separate areas are to be set aside, the settlement now made should, as regards the total area dealt with, be final, so long as the policy of separate areas remains in force. The subject cannot be dealt with by instalments, as the Native cannot in fairness be asked to give up forthwith a right which he possesses in exchange for an immediate instalment of land, to be followed possibly later by a further instalment or instalments, of the value or extent of which no one has any knowledge; moreover from the European standpoint, further instalments at later stages would almost inevitably involve the expropriation of many of them, and a greater expenditure by the State than would be necessitated at present."

CHAPTER IV

THE NATIVE LAND PURCHASER'S "QUID PRO QUO"

A Criticism

CHAPTER IV

["And I said unto them, If ye think good, give me my price; and if not forbear."
ZECHARIAH XI, 12.]

I.

THE QUESTION OF AREAS BEING RESERVED FOR FUTURE CONSIDERATION.

["The subject cannot be dealt with by instalments. . . ."—S. Rhodesian Land Commission, Report, paragraph 103.]

THE Native Land-Purchaser does not appear to me to be getting his fair *quid pro quo* under the Commission's recommendations.

In paragraph 89 the Commission speaks of Europeans in Southern Rhodesia apparently not having fully realized "the fact that the Native has in law the same rights to acquire land as they have, and that when the Reserves were set aside there was no intention whatever of depriving him of that right, and that if he gives up the right to acquire land anywhere, he must secure in return a real *quid pro quo*."

The Commission's Table of Land in Southern Rhodesia in Appendix II, on page 40, gives these details of how much land there is in the Colony:

"Alienated - 31,486,095 acres.
Native Reserves 21,203,498 acres.
Unalienated - 43,529,880 acres."

How does the Commission, roughly speaking, propose to divide this 43½ million acres of available unalienated land between the Europeans and the Natives of Southern Rhodesia ?

The answer is that the Europeans are to have 17,423,815 acres definitely allotted to them at once for their Purchase Areas (see end of paragraph 206). The maximum amount of the Native Purchase Areas recommended by the Commission is considerably less than half that amount which is recommended for European purchase. The new S. Rhodesian census which was taken in April, 1926, has shown the European population to be about 38,200 ; the Native population is estimated on page 19 of the Commissioner's Report at 813,947 ; the ratio of Native population to European population may then be guessed as 20 to 1.

We have the Commission's word for it that : "The majority of the Natives who have expressed an opinion upon the subject, and of the missionaries who have spoken for them, consider that the land should be divided equally. . . ." (See paragraph 81.)

Is that 43½ million acres of Unalienated Land divided equally under the Commission's recommendations ?

Is it divided equitably ? Although it is recommended that the Native's present right to purchase land anywhere should be reformed away at once, while 17 millions and more of acres of land are to be assigned at once for European Areas, and less than half that amount for Native Areas, the Commission recommends that another $17\frac{3}{4}$ million acres of land be reserved *for future consideration.* (See paragraphs 110-116.)

Now when once the Native's present rights are safely repealed—how many of these 17,793,300 acres that are to be left are likely to be allotted to Native Areas—if the local Legislative Assembly in H.M. Colony of Southern Rhodesia is to be the sole allotting authority? One wonders.

Are the 17,423,813 acres now definitely proposed for European Areas to be augmented by the whole of this reservation of 17,793,300 acres at some future date? Is the reservation *for future consideration* of these $17\frac{3}{4}$ million acres, proposed by the Commission, likely to be illusory in practice, and is the real division of the 43 million acres available likely to be in this ratio—35 millions of acres for 40 thousand Europeans, and 8 millions of acres for more than 800 thousand Natives? God forbid!

A memorable warning has been supplied by the experience of the Native population in the Union of South Africa after the Union's Land Act was passed in the year 1913, that it is not well to allow territorial segregation to be legalized in South Africa before the full amount of land intended to be included in Native land-purchase areas be precisely defined.

Did not General Hertzog, the Union of South Africa's Premier, reply thus not long ago to a statement by Sir Thomas Smartt that natives could not live in the limited territory they had then?—" I admit your Native has not been satisfactorily dealt with up to now. When that law was accepted in 1913 it was said to the Natives : 'We are going to give you more than we have assigned to you in these schedules.'"

This acknowledgment of delay to redeem a pledge as to Native land was made about twelve years after the passing of the Segregation Law. In the light of such an acknowledgment, it seems only common-sense to make one clear stipulation before an old-established British principle be bartered away in Southern Rhodesia, and the Native there lose the land-purchase right that he possesses now.

This stipulation is that *at least* half of the 17¾ million acres which the Commission has recommended to be reserved must be definitely earmarked as Native Land before ever Clause 43 be allowed to disappear from the S. Rhodesian Constitution. I am encouraged to know that the Southern Rhodesian Inter-Denominational Missionary Conference, a body of widespread influence, representing the Missions of the Roman Catholic Church, English Church, Wesleyan Methodist Church, Dutch Reformed Church and various Free Church Societies, has declared its willingness to accept the Commission's proposals on two conditions. One is that the amount of land assigned to Natives should be in accordance with the recommendations of the Majority of the Commission[1];

[1] The Land Commission was divided on two important points, both meaning much to the Natives :

(i) The Chairman had Sir Herbert Taylor with him in his recommendation of a substantial augmentation of the total proposed acreage for Native Land-Purchase.

(ii) Sir Herbert Taylor had Mr. Atherstone with him in advising [under a strict interpretation of their Terms of Reference the Commis-

the other is that the $17\frac{3}{4}$ *million acres in question should not be reserved for future consideration, but that they should be divided equally between Europeans and Natives.*

Should the Constitutional change involved in the surrender of Clause 43 be allowed to be effected without any precise stipulation having been secured by the Imperial Government, what share are the natives of Southern Rhodesia likely to be allotted of this big land-balance by the Government of their own Colony?

II.

THE QUESTION OF LARGE COMPACT NATIVE AREAS SUITABLE FOR ADMINISTRATION BY NATIVE COUNCILS.

> [" The extent of Native Areas should be proportioned on a generous scale to the needs of the Native population: a simple obvious proportion which is constantly being lost to view, but which is paramount over every consideration of white self-interest. THE NATIVE MUST HAVE SUFFICIENT LAND IN WHICH TO DEVELOP; FOR ONLY IN THIS WAY CAN HIS FATAL INTERFERENCE WITH THE COURSE OF EUROPEAN DEVELOPMENT BE REMOVED."—ERNEST STUBBS: " Tightening Coils."]

The Report says:

" Another proposal which finds favour with a few witnesses, including two or three who have thought

sioners could not technically recommend] that the important Sabi Reserve in Charter District, Mashonaland, should be definitely allotted in its integrity for the present as a communal Reserve rather than as a Reserve liable to have its acreage reduced by the subtraction of Native Purchase holdings from it. [It should be explained that the Sabi Reserve has had since 1920 an indeterminate future threat of ultimate reduction contingent on railway construction—six miles on each side of a possible railway, with the proviso that existing Native habitations should be respected—hanging over it like a sword of Damocles.] The case for the Majority's findings as against the Minority's on both (i) and (ii) is alike a very strong one. A. S. C.

deeply upon the matter, and who have the interests of the Native much at heart, is that one, or perhaps two, very large areas in Matabeleland and a similar number in Mashonaland should be set apart for Native acquisition, in order that considerable centres of Native life might be formed, which would each be a sphere of action of a Native Council. However great the advantage of such a course might be, we consider that it is impracticable owing to the very heavy expense that would have to be incurred by the Government in acquiring from private owners sufficient land in situations which would satisfy the supporters of this policy. . . ." (See paragraph 120.)

But the Commission answers its own argument to some extent in paragraph 402 of its Report by saying " it is possible that some body such as the Commonwealth Trust or even the Imperial Government might be prepared to advance such part of the necessary funds as the Government of Southern Rhodesia did not feel justified in devoting to the purpose."

Surely the Imperial Government or any private philanthropic body might feel much more disposed to be accommodating towards a model Segregation Scheme of ample " Basutolands " or " Transkeis " than such a piecemeal Scheme as we are presented with by the excellent map of this Report.

That pioneer exponent of Segregation, the late Maurice Evans, wrote : " There must not be small black areas scattered among the whites."

Moreover a well-known publicist, writing of the Union Dominion's Native affairs, has confirmed this opinion recently: "Our experience in the Transkei makes us believe in the segregated areas rather than in the smaller Transvaal type of 'labour reservoirs.'"

I would humbly submit to the Dominions Office that a second-rate Scheme commended with a view to cheapness does *not* promise to make the great and perilous adventure of the establishment of Segregation Areas in a British Colony the attractive and worth-while experiment it should be made.

As evidence that small areas scattered among the whites are *not* likely to have a fair chance to make good, I have only to cite the failure to establish the Transkei Native Council System, from which so much was hoped, in those scattered Native Areas which lie outside the Transkei since the Union Government passed its 1920 Native Affairs Act. As regards Mashonaland it should not be hard to recover that *status quo* of a really large compact Native Territory which the Reserves Order-in-Council (1920) reduced in Districts bordering the Sabi river, and contiguous to that spacious Sabi Reserve, which it threatened to reduce, but which is now ear-marked in its integrity as Native country by the Land Commission.

III.

THE QUESTION OF THE PROPOSED PROHIBITION OF COMMUNAL TENURE IN NATIVE PURCHASE AREAS.

> [" However much we may approve individual title, it seems certain we ought not to force it on any branch of the Abantu. If they desire and seek it, well and good. . . ."—MAURICE EVANS: " Black And White In South Africa, p. 148.]

The Report admits that certain Natives would probably prefer that " land in these areas should be available for purchase by their tribe or a section of their tribe as tribal lands, on communal tenure. Some have definitely asked for this provision, and where Reserves are congested it is a natural and easily understandable desire. It may be mentioned that there is at least one instance of a chief and his people having purchased land in this country in this manner, and it appears in the Land Registry as being so held." (See paragraph 252.)

Thus much for Africans' self-determinant movement towards readjusting legally their immemorial tenure ! But our Commission will have none of it : " We are clearly of opinion that this form of tenure should not be permitted in the Native Purchase Areas." (See paragraph 253.)

Nevertheless the Commission admits that this form of tenure which it proposes to prohibit in Native Purchase Areas respected individual rights, and " in many respects resembled our conception of individual rather than communal tenure." (See paragraphs 238 and 239.)

Is such drastic prohibition as the Commission has advocated really advisable ?

The argument against forcing the pace amongst communally-minded Africans as regards their land tenure has been convincingly developed in that important Nigerian book, " Native Races and their Rulers." Dr. Loram, Native Education Expert in the South African Union, has handled Africa's Tenure question with sympathy and common-sense. He has pointed out that by the time Natives " developed, the Europeans might have arrived at a communal state. Europeans were not necessarily right in everything they had done, nor was it always necessary that the natives should follow them."

Father Burbridge, S.J., an outstanding Rhodesian missionary, testified before this Commission that it was *security* of tenure as well as quality of land, which mattered most to Natives, that (with freehold, State leasehold, and Communal tenures respectively) Africans in Transkei, Nigeria and Basutoland had alike made good. The late Maurice Evans, C.M.G., in " Black and White in South-East Africa," said of Communal tenure : " What would be fatal to the best results if applied to Europeans does not bar success when continued by Natives—the custom is their own, and under circumstances otherwise favourable they do not feel its drawbacks and restraints."

This Rhodesian Commission's proposal to prohibit Communal tenure in Purchase Areas for Natives is unconvincing when we recall Sir Godfrey Lagden's testimony as to communally-farmed Basutoland. " *No white population could produce as much in the space available.*"

"I am not opposing individual tenure." So wrote Maurice Evans: he admitted that "to some extent it is inevitable; provision must be made for many who have fully accepted the way of the white man. I want to emphasize here again the different angle from which black and white view life. . . ."

While encouraging the de-tribalized Native to purchase an isolated holding, let us pause before we actively discourage a section of a Native Tribe from purchasing a block of land and holding it together. This is a grave matter of State—this question of legal interference with honourable and immemorial tradition.

I submit that (1) it is unreasonable to prevent a number of individuals from clubbing together to buy a farm, (2) it is wrong to override Native custom, unless such interference be obviously for the Native's benefit.

Supplemental Note.

I am indebted to an experienced member of the Southern Rhodesian Native Department for the arguments that follow.

A. S. C.

A Plea for Tolerance of Communal Tenure in the Proposed Native Land-Purchase Areas.

I am of opinion that it is tremendously important carefully to consider the question of individual and communal tenure. One cannot lightly set aside traditions and institutions centuries old. Natives have undoubtedly succeeded in community and it is very questionable whether they will do so equally individually; many will certainly make good, but many will fail. Their old system of assisting one another in their agricultural and other pursuits is a splendid asset and a precious institution. It incidentally solves the labour problem, one does not hear among them the frequent wail of the Europeans " shortage of labour."

However suitable the recommended purchase areas may be, it is obvious they cannot all be good land and will not lend themselves to be cut up into small holdings of a suitable nature. Some purchasers will get plums, others snags. The position will be exactly as with the European with small capital and poor land; he cannot make good. As a community the natives will have facilities to progress and prosper; as individuals they will experience difficulties and probably fail. I am, therefore, strongly of opinion that their interests will be best served if communal tenure is permitted whenever desired.

Recently I have heard of an application by an educated married man in employment. He had decided on a big area in some district. In the application he stated that his father and four sons (of whom applicant is one), were all in employment in various parts of the Colony and that, to use his own expression, " the whole family would sacrifice itself to acquire this particular area." Here is evidence, what does it convey ?

In the past, Companies have taken up huge areas, the

pick of the land; many have locked up such land to this day. How different the position would be if Natives had been able to acquire some of them. These would have been speedily and well populated, progress and prosperity reigning, contentment and a sense of security achieved: " The realization and joy of a permanent home."

We cannot change old time traditions, and, even under changed conditions, we must recognize and foster the good and successful ones, rather than curb them.

" The true path is to guide Evolution of primitive races by methods based on their own customs."—(Sir F. Lugard.)

IV.

The Question of an Easy Instalments Purchase System in the proposed Native Areas.

[" And strong compulsion plucks the scrap from pride ;
But still that scrap is bought with many a sigh,
And pride embitters what it can't deny."
—Crabbe : " The Village."]

Why should leasehold be prohibited in the proposed Native Areas ? Why should settling down on a piece of ground have been made so easy for the European settler in the past, and why is it now to be made so hard for the Native in a Native Purchase Area ? Why it cannot be recommended that Natives should be allowed to settle on the land in Native Purchase Areas —with a Permit of Occupation Tenure—pledged to pay off a minimum instalment of the purchase price each year, I fail to see. Why the Native must pay the whole purchase price down and also commute for quit-rent before being allowed access to land in a *Native* Purchase Area (Paragraphs 260, 261, 262), it is hard to comprehend. This is racial differentiation with a vengeance.

V.

THE QUESTION OF SECURING THAT NATIVE LAND-PURCHASE SHOULD BE PUT ON THE FOOTING OF ORDINARY BRITISH LAND-PURCHASE SAVE ONLY IN REGARD TO THE LIMITATION OF A NATIVE'S RIGHT TO RAISE MONEY ON MORTGAGE.

["I . . . greatly wish to ease his lot by all possible means—except by getting off his back."
TOLSTOY.]

I would submit that such pin-prick racial differentiation proposals as are indicated in paragraphs 264[1] and 319[2] should be definitely renounced, as likely

[1] A quotation may be given: "If it were practicable we should prefer to see a title given only to such portion of the land as was from time to time brought under cultivation or stocked with a suitable number of cattle or small stock."

[2] The Commission recommends that "regulations should be enacted from time to time as may be found practicable to prohibit in these areas the keeping of Native or scrub bulls or at least . . ." Its alternative suggestion may be a tolerable one, but what shall be said of the one I have quoted in full? One has heard of even a Native bull being a fine beast; one has heard of a European cattle-breeder setting himself to improve our hardy and serviceable Native cattle by selection in one District of Mashonaland. A recent Report of the Tanganyika Territory contains a section on "Animal Husbandry," which will repay study: "The stock districts were searched for suitable native sires and with the importation of an Ayrshire and a Friesland

to prejudice a Policy of Racial Segregation Areas at the very outset. My contention is that, difficult though it may be for the Southern Rhodesian Native to purchase land under the right which Clause 43 of our Constitution guarantees to him, nevertheless, when once he has achieved land-purchase under the present system, he has obtained something that is really worth his while to him, while under the arbitrary interference by back-veld Bumbledom, which is foreshadowed by some of the Commission's proposals for Native Purchase Areas, it would be indeed questionable whether land-purchase would be a reality, and worth the Native's while. After reading some of the Commission's canny proposals one is inclined to put a question and to expect an answer :

Question. When is Freedom of Land-Purchase not Freedom ?

Answer. When it is Freedom of *Native* Land-Purchase.

I would submit that the Home Government ought to be itself represented on such a Land-Purchase Board for Native Purchase as the Commission recommends should be created.

bull from Kenya, a start was made. . . ." The Report goes on to speak of selected indigenous as well as selected imported sires. It tells us that in " crossing the breeds the natural qualities of the various types of native stock are studied. For instance, in crossing cattle from the Ugogo country and Masailand with imported stock, it is sought, while increasing the milking properties of the herd, to preserve the natural hardiness of the breed in the arid thorn-covered country in which it lives. Similarly with the Iringa cattle the object is to improve the beef type without impairing the natural suitability of the breed for the poorer districts of the Territory."

VI.

The Question of Natives living in European Areas

> [" If they are allowed to remain on the land, do they have to pay rent to the new proprietor, work for him—or both—and thus become virtually his serfs ? "—Edwin Smith : " The Christian Mission In Africa."]

Under the Land Commission's recommendations what will be the conditions for Natives on farms ?

This is a very important question indeed in H.M. Colony of Southern Rhodesia. Out of a population of Natives estimated by the Commission at 813,947, only 516,335 were estimated to be living in Native Reserves. It does seem that some determined effort ought to be made to secure that the conditions for Natives in European Areas be not unduly tightened up upon the inauguration of a Segregation Areas Policy in Southern Rhodesia. I would commend the suggestion of the Rev. W. A. Cotton, C.R., made in " The Race Problem in South Africa " (with a view to mitigating the conditions for Natives in the European Areas of the S. African Union)—that " the bar against leasehold tenancy of land by Natives should be removed wherever they were admitted as labourers."

An important paper advocating a leasehold tenure for Natives in European Areas was read by Mr. J. D. Rheinallt Jones, at that European-Bantu Conference which was convoked by the Federal Council of the Dutch Reformed Churches in Cape Town. (Jan. and Feb., 1927.)

VII.

The Question of some Alternative Course being taken if the waiving of Clause 43 be considered for the present unadvisable.

> [" I cannot support any detraction from existing rights. In any case to confine the right in land of the Natives of the soil to less than half the country, though they are far more in number than immigrants, is obviously indefensible. I cannot think it likely that the report will ever be translated into legislation."—Private letter from an Independent Labour Party Publicist.]

I would submit that if it should be found impracticable to obtain an amicable settlement on the lines of the dropping of Clause 43, some attempt should be made alike to alleviate Native land-hunger, and to obviate inter-racial friction, by encouraging Natives to buy land near those existing tribal Reserves, the total acreage of which was so lamentably reduced in the year 1920. After this manner the beneficent process of natural race gravitation may be brought into play, and Natives may gladly seize upon facilities for taking up suitable land in Native neighbourhoods. A passage in the Land Commission's Report (see Paragraph 69) ought, I maintain, to be given full consideration in the event of no change in the Colony's Responsible Government Constitution being considered feasible, and of any decisive ruling that Clause 43 be left as it is :

" In view . . . of the rights of the Native under the Constitution, it is urged that in the event of no amendment to the Constitution taking place, if there be any doubt on the subject it be removed, and that the Government should set aside suitable areas of Crown land in which the Native would be welcomed as a purchaser, especially in view of the fact that the inquiries made by the Commission will undoubtedly have made known for the first time to many of the Natives their rights to purchase land, and will have inspired a hope in many of them that land will be made available for purchase by them in the future ; and consequently considerable dissatisfaction and discontent would almost inevitably arise if nothing were done in this direction."

CHAPTER V

IF SEGREGATION AREAS ARE TO HAVE A TRIAL IN THE BRITISH EMPIRE, WHY SHOULD THEY NOT BE GIVEN A FAIR TRIAL?

CHAPTER V

> "Oh if we draw a circle premature
> Heedless of far gain,
> Greedy for quick returns of profit, sure
> Bad is our bargain."
>
> R. BROWNING.

BRIEFLY stated, my view is that those of us who care for the Native Races' future in this great Territory had better be prompt in accepting a compromise and surrendering Clause 43 on terms, if only the terms which have been offered to us can be amended satisfactorily. But I wish here to stress the extraordinary solemn responsibility that rests upon those who wish the Natives well at this crisis in our Colony's history. Clause 43 has huge potentialities as to the future, if insignificant effectiveness at this present moment of time. Let us remember that in considering the interests of Southern Rhodesia's Natives we are considering the interests of eight hundred and thirteen thousands of our fellow British subjects. Let us remember, in reckoning out the due proportion of the land proposed to be devoted to them and to their children, the proportion of their numbers to the number of the settlers, also what a mighty proportion of the whole Southern Rhodesian revenue they pay,[1] also what proportion of all the manual labour supplied in the Territory they are accustomed to supply.[2]

In Mr. Edwin Smith's "The Golden Stool" we are told that the Native is "in some colonies made to contribute more than his share to the public revenue, and in effect subsidizes the European settlement." It is arguable that S. Rhodesia is one of those colonies.

On behalf of a model Scheme, and such a Scheme alone, ought we to be able to appeal confidently to our Imperial Government to find means to enable a Colonial Government with comparatively small funds at its disposal to help it into being. We use the expression "help into being" advisedly. After a time the Native Areas may be expected to provide a substantial return for initial outlay. Our Commission says of its own recommended Scheme in paragraph 404:

[1] It should be remembered that any Native boy of about fourteen years of age under the present regime may be called upon to pay a poll-tax of £1 a year as an adult male, when his wage-earning capacity is only approximately 5s. a month and rations—the Administration's claim to an iniquitous exercise of discretion as to the interpretation of "adult male" having been handed on from B.S.A. Co. days. The Colonial Secretary of S. Rhodesia wrote under date of Dec. 30th, 1926: "Alone among wage-earners in Southern Rhodesia, the natives' wages are not greater than the average pre-war rates."

[2] There is an idea that Southern Rhodesia's employers largely depend upon outside labour. Nevertheless the Land Commission notes that the indigenous Native Labour supply has increased from 28,701 in 1910 to 49,800 in 1924, and that (the average of employment periods being about four months) it was estimated that 150,000 came out to work in 1924. Mr. Leggate, M.L.A., Colonial Secretary, writing at the end of 1926, said: "so far as indigenous natives are concerned, the census which has just been taken shows that they contribute a reasonable proportion of their numbers towards the supply of labour to white settlers," the word "reasonable" being interpreted according to the standards which have been applied to all the British territories between the Cape and Abyssinia. On 2nd May, 1927, H.E. the Governor said: "Our Native subjects have been loyal and law-abiding. . . . Natives employed shows an increase in round figures from 52,000 in 1921, to 78,000 in 1926—a 50 per cent. advance."

"The revenue which will ultimately result to the Government from the adoption of a policy of separate areas will be very considerable."

Imperial help in promoting Segregation Areas to encourage Southern Rhodesia's inter-racial goodwill may enlist the hearty support of some Imperialists whom an appeal for Imperial loans to multiply such luxuries as new railways in Kenya[1] leaves cold.

The Policy of Segregation Areas is worth trying as a remedy for grave and complex maladies in the African part of our Empire: necessities should take precedence of luxuries.

But the ship of a great Imperial relief venture should not be ruined by parsimony about penn'orths of tar. If large compact areas of the Basutoland type, quarter-Basutolands[2] or half-Basutolands, would give the Mashonaland and Matabele tribes a far better chance than comparatively small and severed Native Purchase Areas, then the Recommendations of this Report need to be amended in important particulars. Expropriation is doubtless an expensive Policy, but the Commission has voted for at least some Expropriation. A first-rate Expropriation Policy may commend itself as worth Imperial backing where a mere second-class makeshift scheme (with an illusory

[1] "Too long has the Imperial System been regarded 'as a gigantic storehouse of outdoor relief for the aristocracy'—to use the words of John Bright. It is time that someone else should get a chance. There is the principle of equality of opportunity. We might try the principle here, for a change."—Mr. Robert Chamberlain, quoted in N. Leys' "Kenya" (page 134, 3rd edition).

[2] Basutoland is stated to contain 3,112,297 morgen (a morgen being 2⅛ acres). Half of all the unalienated land in the Colony (approximately 43 million acres) should provide some three Basutolands in extent for Native Southern Rhodesia.

attraction of cheapness) may fail to excite enthusiasm outside the borders of the Colony concerned. A Segregation Policy, if it be worth trying, is worth trying well. We are not so rich in alternative expedients as to be able to court failure in this experiment of Territorial Segregation that we in South Africa propose to take the responsibility of making. The Land Question is a mightily serious[1] question in our part of Africa. A comparatively equitable Segregation Scheme of compact Areas, a Scheme pledged to no tyrannous orthodoxy about enforcing European tenure, a Scheme rising superior to the temptation to multiply petty regulations (that so easily besets experiments of the sort in our own day), may do much to give a convincing assurance of good faith as to the Land Question.

By its aid African Native life may be given room to develop on its own African lines—a consummation most devoutly to be wished for: in this way two outstanding British-ruled African Races, Mashona and Matabele, may be granted a fairer chance than ever before to bring their peculiar and unique contributions, each of them, their Racial Glory and Tribal Honour, into the Treasury of the City of God.

But we have had our warnings in Africa not to be dilatory in these matters, not to tread the primrose

[1] " This thing that is the *fons et origo mali* is the constant dread that we (the Europeans) are going to eat up their land. If a Kafir could give expression to his fears he would say ' the land's the thing ; *that* is the touchstone that shows the real attitude of the white man towards the black. If . . . South Africa could but put the native mind at rest on this point, the trouble that is fermenting everywhere would soon disappear ' ; but somehow our assurances do not assure the Kafirs."—(Dudley Kidd, " Kafir Socialism.")

path of dalliance to the everlasting bonfire of our might-have-beens.

Time presses. We are just now at cross-roads. Soon, should we choose a road other than that we might well have followed, relentless Space may divide us irrevocably from such a goal of give-and-take goodwill as some of us doubtless suppose we have every intention of reaching. *Now* there would seem to be hope to reach such a goal, hope for both Races, Europe's and Africa's.

To quote well-known words with but little adaptation :

> " There is a tide in the affairs of men
> That, taken at the flood, leads on to fortune ;
> Omitted, all the voyage of their Race
> Is bound in shallows and in miseries."

AFTER-WORD

THIS book has asked attention for the Native African's point of view.

It seems right, then, in discussing an African Land Question to allow an African Welfare Association to have the last word of all in its pages.

The general secretary (A. M. Zigode) of the S. Rhodesia Native Welfare Association states "that the following resolutions were passed for submission to the Government at a recent conference held in Gwelo :

(1) That in connection with the Native Land Bill the Association could not agree with the report of the Commission, pending thorough investigation.

(2) That the Bantu chiefs, in their evidence, had really meant cutting the Colony into two equal portions for black and white.

(3) That the Government be asked to appoint a fresh Land Commission.

(4) That the British act and principle lays down fair play as between the races—equal justice, equal opportunity to rise, and equal right to this common land.

(5) That most of the farms in the new proposed area for natives are quite dry and very unfertile, and the area in question would be far too small for the natives concerned.

(6) That the difficulty of the whole matter is the unsatisfactory position with regard to native squatters; this is a Bill to make provision for the settlement of the native squatters' question by providing land on a place to which they may go, if they are removed from the farms where they are now.

(7) That Parliament has no right to deprive the natives of the land, under Clause 43, Government Gazette Extraordinary, dated 18th January, 1922."

(See *The Gwelo Times*, April 15th, 1927.)

INDEX OF PERSONS MENTIONED OR QUOTED